ACKNOWLEDGEMENTS

Jeannette for company, campsites and *campesino* fayre.
Alud for replacing the irreplaceable.

CONTENTS

1. Sierra de Orihuela 21
2. Sierra de Callosa de Segura 29
3. Sierra de Crevillente 35
4. Two short walks in the Campo de Alicante 40
    a. Sierra de las Aguilas 40
    b. PR189 Barranco de Berlandi 43
5. Sierra del Cid 47
6. Sierra de Maigmo 53
7. Penya Migjorn 61
8. Sierra de Cabezón d'Oro or Cabeçó d'Or 67
9. Cami de la Bacorera 73
10. El Faro del Albir & Punta Bombarda 79
11. Sierra Helada (linear traverse) 83
12. Puig Campana 89
    ALTERNATIVE SHORT WALK: Sierra Cortina 92
13. Barrancos del Arc & Charquer 97
14. PR198 Alto de la Penya de Sella 103
15. Cumbre de Aitana 111
16. PR15 Barranco del Salt 117
17. Monte Ponoig from Finestrat 123
18. Sierra de Aixorta 129

19. Sierra de Bèrnia...137

20. The Breasts On The Sunny Side Of The Mountain.....143

21. Castell de Aixa..151

22. Sierra de Segaria..157

23. Penyal d'Ifac 163

24. Sierra d'Oltà 167

25. Caves, Capes, Castles & Cliffs - four coastal strolls..173

    a. Cova Tallada & Torre de Gerro 173

    b. Far de Sant Antoni 176

    c. Castillo de Granadella 177

    d. Torre Vigia de Cap d'Or & Cova de la Cendre 180

26. El Montgo 183

27. Penyo Roig from Murla 189

28. PR.158 Sierra del Carrascal de Parcent....................195

29. Barrancs de Racons and l'Infern................................201

30. Refugio de la Figuereta via Travesia el Masset 207

31. Barranc de l'Infern 211

32. Two small walks, two large valleys:

    a. Gallinera & Alcalá 217

    b. Penya Foradada..220

33. Raco del Duc...225

Torre del Gerro

INTRODUCTION

Mixing Metaphors:
The Protean Costa Blanca

The **Costa Blanca** has more sierras than a sawmill. Carve some of Spain's most famous valleys between the sierras, riddle the rock with enough cavities to keep a dental school busy for decades, lace the heights with hundreds of waymarked trails, embroider the coast with cliffs, coves and beaches, then link the lot together with a network of winding mountain roads boasting more kinks than a bagful of Slinkies, and you've got a metaphor sufficiently mixed to match the diverse charms of this enchanting region.

Like most mixed metaphors, this is not merely sloppy writing, but an attempt to suggest the richness of a landscape that can assume a variety of disguises depending on how you approach it. Smeared with one of the Mediterranean's more surreal concentrations of tower blocks and dotted with theme parks that only serve to highlight the sense of unreality, the Costa Blanca has long been a byword for mass tourism. Alicante has lost all the exotic overtones of its Moorish past and the mere mention of Benidorm is enough to trigger a Pythonesque rant about the sort of holiday in which it's the tourist rather than the services that are packaged. This is the land of the triple S's, sun, sand, and sea, and if that's what you're after, it's there in abundance.

But this clichéd facade masks a multiplicity of Costa Blancas, each appealing to a different public: there's the easy living and benign climate that lure pensioners for the Winter season; the fabulous countryside and affordable housing that have attracted countless second-home owners; the rich cultural heritage that entices cognoscenti of historic architecture and picturesque customs; the evocative mythological landscape that has been responsible for many a migrant losing themselves in dreams of a fantastical Spain; and a culinary tradition, irresistible to gourmets and gourmands alike, that has gone some way to defining what it is to be Spanish. Above all though, there is the Costa Blanca of paths.

Like nothing else, the path is the quintessence of Spain and its gregarious traditions. Every farmhouse in Spain, no matter how far-flung, will have a path beaten to the next household, every hamlet, no matter how remote or strongly fortified, will have an ancient trail leading to the next village, and what neighbours have seen fit to instigate, shepherds, packmen, muleteers, snow-gatherers, pilgrims, charcoal-burners, limefirers, foresters, hunters, coastguards, soldiers, engineers, aristocrats, even empires and invaders, and latterly tourist conscious local authorities and health promoting governments have confirmed.

Nowhere is this truer than on the Costa Blanca. In recent years, hundreds of old paths have been waymarked or brought under the protective aegis of the 'Vias Verdes' (Green Ways) classification, and more are being cleaned, waymarked and signposted all the time. It is this Costa Blanca, the Costa Blanca of paths, that is celebrated in the present publication. Forget the tower blocks, the discos, the themed pubs, the castles in the air and the simulacrum of home-plus-sun, and take a step beyond the clichés into a small paradise, a place of improbable crags, dramatic summits, deep gorges and great paths, a place, in short, where the walker is king.

THE WHO AND THE WHAT:
target market and geographic range

This is **a gateway book**, designed to take newcomers into an unknown landscape, encourage long term residents to a deeper exploration of what lies behind the coast, and give an idea of what's possible when you take a step away from the packaged tour and processed dreams.

Any book pretending to be a definitive guide to the region's walks would be lying - either in its claims or simply on the ground because it would be too heavy to pick up. If you think you 'know' all the walks, you're probably wrong and probably won't have read this far anyway. If you know that any worthwhile landscape is capable of infinite exploration and it's handy to have a guide for the preliminary investigation, then this is the book for you.

The **object** is to give an overview of what's possible, not merely presenting a series of discrete itineraries but suggesting other ways into a given mountain, so that you end each walk knowing that's just the start, that there are alternative routes to be discovered and that each walk is a prelude rather than a conclusion. Forget about been-there-done-that. This is been-there-going-again-because-it's-good.

The **walks** are all *walks* and require no special equipment, though in one or two cases the definition of walking may be extended to include knees, hands and even bottoms! There are several short walks for those who just want to potter about within sight of the sea, over a dozen summits for the peak-baggers, and enough rough, occasionally off-path itineraries to satisfy the more exigent hiker, but by far the greater number of routes are pitched at the averagely fit hill-walker, and if that seems a tad ambitious, **short versions** and **strolls** are included for less energetic outings.

For obvious reasons, the **coastal definition** is a little fluid, as there's only so much time even the most indomitable rambler is ready to spend hopping over garden fences and squeezing past skyscrapers. There are half a dozen walks actually on the coast, the rest are generally in the first ranges of mountains in the hinterland. As a rough guideline, we aimed for all walks to start within 10 kilometres of the coast as the crow flies, though it might not always be evident where precisely the crow's flying from, and I've felt free to extend this area to include walks that would otherwise have been arbitrarily excluded.

The most obvious exceptions to the 10 kilometre rule are the walks behind Alicante, where good road links shrink the distance, and to the south, where a stricter definition of coastal would have you floundering about in the salt marshes. Inevitably, anyone familiar with the area will look at the contents and start huffing and puffing and gasping, "But he hasn't done...". Great walking areas round places like Alcoi and Sax have been excluded as being just too far inland to qualify for the *costa* definition, but hopefully there are enough classic walks and enough novel itineraries to satisfy newcomers and old hands alike.

WHEN TO GO WHAT TO TAKE

The best months for a dedicated walking holiday are March to May and September to November. October's traditionally the wettest month, but like everywhere else, the weather's doing some funny things in Spain, and October was the driest month of the year when we researched this book. There's good walking to be had throughout the Winter, though it is possible for several days of low cloud and rain to keep you off the higher ranges. Summer walks are effectively restricted to early morning or the evening, though some Northerners do seem inclined to mimic toast and you will see the occasional

"Mad dogs and Englishmen..."

hardy soul labouring through the blazing midday heat. Noel Coward had something to say about that.

Most walks can be undertaken with nothing more than a windbreaker and/or fleece/jumper, though it's worth taking a light waterproof for those days when rain threatens. Thorny scrub often means long trousers are preferable to shorts, while stony ground can make walking sandals a liability. If you're travelling light, a pair of trainers or walking shoes will do for most itineraries, though boots are nearly always better. A hat is advisable.

Most itineraries can be done in the space of a morning, ending with lunch at a restaurant, but given the time involved in getting to the start then actually enjoying the walk (there's no point racing round simply to keep an appointment with your tummy), I recommend taking a picnic for any walk timed at more than three hours, and even the two hour walks can easily fill a long half day with a leisurely picnic en route. Always take plenty of water (1 litre per person is a basic minimum, more for longer walks and in hot weather) and don't rely on *fuentes*, which may be dry or siphoned off for purposes more commercially rewarding than rehydrating an expiring rambler.

HOW TO GET THERE, GET ABOUT, GET A BED AND GET FED

Telling you **how to get there** may seem like breathtaking condescension, given that tens of thousands of people have been flying into Alicante airport on package deals and charters for the last forty years, and this remains the cheapest and simplest option. However, if you have the time, the rewards of **driving** across Spain are infinite, as in many parts of the hinterland the ultramodern progressive state that has emerged since the death of Franco is still only a veneer slapped onto an older grittier world untouched by the imperatives of conventional tourism, while the winding mountain roads (ideal for motorcycles) will turn your head and your heart as well as your stomach. I've been ploughing back and forth across the country for fifteen years, and still take to the road with a sense of happy expectation. Regular ferry services connect Britain with Bilbao and Santander, after which if you stick to the backroads, I can almost guarantee an extraordinary trip.

Arriving with your own vehicle also solves the problem of **getting about**, since private transport is still the best way to access most of the interesting walks without spending hours trudging along tarmac lanes and dusty tracks or, worse still, traversing acres of soulless housing complexes. A local train runs along the coast between Alicante and Denia, and most coastal areas have good bus connections, but many inland *pueblos* only have a twice daily service geared more to workers coming down to the coast than ramblers going up to the mountains. If you don't have your own vehicle, a hire car is recommended.

Getting a bed is as blindingly obvious as getting a flight. Unless you come in the height of Summer, finding somewhere to stay on the spot is not a problem, except in some of the camping complexes around Benidorm, to which entire villages of Brits, Dutch, Belgians or Germans (the nationality may vary according to the site) decamp for the season.

Benidorm

Getting fed in Spain is nearly always light on the pocket and palate, though it may prove heavier when you consider trivial matters like cholesterol, weight, and the state of your waistline. If you want full English breakfasts, fish and chips, roast and two veg, and the great British curry, the influx of foreign visitors guarantees you can get them. If you want a taste of Spain, a grand culinary tradition of 'hearty' (as in heartburn if you tend to gluttony) peasant cooking awaits.

The Valencian *Paella* needs no introduction, though it should be noted that the Spanish wouldn't dream of eating it in the evening, and if you find yourself in a restaurant that offers it as a dish for one rather than a minimum of two people, it's probably best avoided. Most restaurants will have a range of paella style dishes going under different names, notably *Arroz Negro,* 'black' rice because cooked in squid's ink. Varieties of sausage abound, including *longaniza, chorizo, salchichon* and *morcilla* or *butifarra negra,* a black pudding that makes the English version look positively anaemic.

The best meat is lamb (*cordero* or *agnell*), butchered younger than in England, which is all to the good. The same phenomenon is all to the bad with beef, which tends to be *ternera,* a variety of elderly veal. Pork (*cerdo*) varies between good and indifferent, depending on provenance, but the popularity of hams (*jamon*) from mast fattened pigs means few cuts (*chuletas* are chops, *lomo* a tenderloin) are liable to dissolve into a milky looking puddle of steroids. *Olla* is a casserole (every village has its own variety), *albondigas* are meat balls, nearly always homemade (*casero/a* or *de la casa*), *jabali* is wild boar, and *choto* kid.

With the decline of rural poverty and increasing standards of living, a 'Spanish vegetarian meal' has become a humorous oxymoron, but a long tradition of stews based round a variety of pulses (lentils/*lentejas,* chick peas/*garbanzos,* dry beans/*judias*) means the basic know-how is there, albeit often embellished with a generous lump of lard! Otherwise, vegetarians will find themselves eating a lot of soup (steer clear of the *picadillo,* which is stock garnished with ham) and eggs, including the famous *tortilla* (qualified as being *Francesa* if it's an ordinary omelette) and *revueltos* (eggs scrambled with vegetables).

Finally, it's worth mentioning two ideal picnic foods produced by local bakeries: *coca* is a type of pizza found throughout the Catalan speaking lands and very good, too; *empandillas* or *bollos* are pasties filled with meat and egg, spinach, chard, tuna or *pisto,* a tomato and pepper mix also used as a topping on *coca.*

FINDING YOUR WAY...
ON THE GROUND AND IN THE BOOK

The Spanish are a generous hearted people, nowhere more so than in their walking, and the Costa Blanca is one of the country's most munificent regions when it comes to **waymarked paths**. In case you're unfamiliar with the system GRs (*Gran Recorridos*) are long distance paths of 50 kilometres or more, waymarked with red and white stripes. The only significant one in Alicante Province, the GR7, is beyond our area, though there are some paths that use GR waymarking nearer the coast. SLs (*Senderos Locales*) are linking paths, less than 10 kilometres long, waymarked green and white. But the paths at which the Costa Blanca excels, are the PRs (*Pequeños Recorridos*), 'short' walks taking between one and two days, and waymarked yellow and white. To give you an idea of just how rich the region is in PRs, my preliminary list of potential walks for this book had over 160 itineraries!

Many **PRs** display a disastrous affinity for tarmac (whether as a result of laziness on the part of the man with the pot of paint or an overzealous respect on the part of the local authorities for otherwise untenanted private land, I don't know), while others are linear routes that take no account of public transport, but this is still an extraordinary resource, and I hope this book will encourage you to exploit the network to the full once you're familiar with the system. As a rule, when part of a route can be driven, we drive it, outlining the drivable bit in the Getting To The Start précis. When a walk follows a PR in its entirety, the PR number will appear in the walk title. Where a section of a longer PR constitutes our entire itinerary, the fact will be mentioned in the introductory note or list of other walks in the area. When a PR is crossed or used only briefly, the information will appear in the walk description.

Nearly every tourist office and *ayuntamiento* will have some **printed matter about walking**. If you insist on it being in English, the chances are you'll get a sorry looking leaflet and a very sketchy sketch map. But if you can muddle your way through Spanish or, better still, *Valenciano* (depending on which side of the border you happen to be born, this is either a dialect of Catalan or a language in its own right; either way, it's easy to read if you know a little French and Spanish), you may be deluged with pamphlets and booklets. Even if you can't read the lingo, these generally include maps giving you an idea of alternative walks. The official data on mapboards and signposts may sound precise, but is frequently inaccurate: distances are often overestimated, times underestimated.

If following **unofficial waymarked paths** (which usually opt for dots and arrows rather than stripes), beware of mistaking boundary markers for waymarks. The former often use brighter more synthetic colours, but are not always distinguishable from waymarks. Another give-away is that they tend to be more frequent and are accompanied by numbers, letters, symbols, or arrows indicating something manifestly unwalkable. On the whole, this is not one of those areas of Spain (and there are many), where waymarked paths will have you clinging to a clump of dead rosemary loosely set in a crumbling escarpment over a 200 metre drop. That said, some cairns and waymarks only indicate climbers' paths.

Don't dismiss outwardly unappealing areas simply because of their aspect or because there are no famous walks there. The bare brown hills behind and between Campello and Villajoyosa, for example, look downright deadly on a hot day, but gilded by the bright golden light of a winter sunset or washed with a recent shower when the mountains are shrouded in cloud, they have the makings of many delightful strolls. Beware, though, if walking with a dog since these hills serve as a hatchery and hunters lay poison in Spring to protect fledgling partridge from strays and foxes.

Hopefully, **finding your way in the book** is obvious. Walks are divided by area to aid location and numbered from south to north. Each itinerary is preceded by an introduction describing the type of walk and noting any difficulties encountered en route. A fact file summarizes times, climbs, distances, difficulty, and means of access, plus suggestions for strolls and/or short versions. To help with the expressed 'gateway' objective, the *resumé* is followed by a list of other waymarked routes in the vicinity, alternative points of access, and occasionally a brief description of an alternative walk.

I usually walk with a laptop in my rucksack, effectively doubling the weight of an ordinary day pack. You may do stretches of a given path quicker than I timed them, but it's unlikely you'll finish the entire route in less than my global time. Add 15' per hour for snacking, snapping and standing still staring. If you do find yourself completing a walk in less time, you may care to consult a psychiatrist or take up a more competitive leisure activity.

Place names on maps and signs vary, sometimes appearing in Spanish, other times in *Valenciano*. When there's little risk of confusion (Calpe/Calp), I stick with the Spanish. When there's a significant difference (Jalon/Xalo), I note both names then use the one I saw used most often on the ground. Geographical features appearing on the Military Maps are given the name used there, except when local usage is totally at variance. I've tried to avoid peppering the text with names that don't appear on the maps, except where the names describe a celebrated feature or something cited on signposts.

FLORA AND FAUNA

As elsewhere in Spain, the mountains are one massive herb garden, awash with thyme, rosemary, oregano, and a host of pungent flowering plants that would baffle most English cooks. Wildflowers are varied and frequently specific to a locale, as evidenced by the plethora of '*microreservas*' dotted about in the most implausible places. A good field guide is indispensable. Though premised on observations in Andalucia, Betty Molesworth-Allen's Wildflowers of Southern Spain (Santana) is an ideal introductory guide, clearly identifying the classic flora found throughout the Mediterranean.

Birds of prey (sparrow hawks, kestrel and peregrine falcons) are common in the mountains, Hoopoe and bee-eaters are regular visitors across the province, while flamingoes grace the salt marshes in the south, and the rare Audouin gull can be seen on the coast. On the ground, there are wild boar, fox, badger, ibex, and genet, but you'll probably only see the first two, and the chances are the boar will be on a plate in a sauce.

POTENTIAL PROBLEMS

Judging by the security personnel in campsites, commercial centres and *urbanizaciones*, petty crime is rife, but anecdotal evidence suggests it is only petty and I've not heard of anyone encountering anything more disagreeable than a sneak thief. Watch your bag in superstores and when loading your car, and you shouldn't have any problems. If a young man in a city offers to keep an eye (albeit a slightly unfocussed eye) on your car for a small consideration, do not refuse, even if you've already bought a ticket.

Spain is still largely owned by people who wouldn't understand the function of a 'No Trespassing' notice even if it came with a video demonstration (and if they did, their countrymen would probably treat the sign as a negation of the very concept of trespass rather than a prohibition), though the sheer numbers of visitors to the Costa Blanca has engendered a rash of *'camino privado'* signs. Access is not generally a problem though and there are so many waymarked paths, you're unlikely to find yourself short of walks unless you have very hungry legs indeed.

More problematic in the general scheme of things is the mentality, rife along all the Spanish *costas,* that seeks to reduce landscape to real estate and regards a mountain as nothing more than a rather superior foundation for a few villas with sea views. Tap 'Costa Blanca' into a search engine and there's every chance you'll come away concluding it's some esoteric code exchanged between shady estate agents unwilling to otherwise expose themselves to the light of day. Fortunately, local nature lovers and outward bound enthusiasts have realized the dangers of dumping holiday homes all over the place and are extremely active, promoting waymarked paths, agitating for reclassification of rural areas to preserve them from the bulldozer boys, and volunteering their services for maintaining the countryside and clearing old paths. In the unlikely event that you do find one of our itineraries cut by a building project (we've tried to avoid areas at risk), please let us know.

WHAT TO DO ON A DAY OFF FROM WALKING

Entertainments on the coast are obvious (sometimes a little too obvious) and heavily promoted, but if you want to get off the beaten track without beating one for yourself, the ideal way to spend a day off walking is to do one of the drives featured in Derek Workman's informative book, <u>Inland Trips From The Costa Blanca</u> (Santana).

The steep descent

1. Sierra de Orihuela

Time:	4h
Climb:	675 metres
Distance:	11.5km
Grade:	medium/difficult
Access:	by car
Stroll:	Rincon de Bonanza *área recreativa*, turning left at the 13M mark to return to the start
Short Version:	San Cristobal

The flatlands to the south of Alicante are a sorry looking proposition in walking terms, until that is you head inland and are confronted by the dramatic dolomite and limestone ridges of the Sierra de Orihuela and it's neighbour, the Sierra de Callosa de Segura. Rising out of the tidy tapestry of domestic farmland like the humped backs of great slumbering beasts these two fabulous little ranges are the sort of places to have any sane rambler salivating and strapping on the boots, muttering, "Yup, gotta get up there".

In this itinerary we tackle the larger of the two, the Sierra de Orihuela. At first glance, this fine mountain seems a tad inaccessible, ringed by major roads, half-built *urbanizaciones* and a population with an unparalleled penchant for fly-tipping. However, once you get past these impedimenta, the mountain is a marvellous place with some beautifully waymarked trails, the latter amounting to a work of art.

Seen on the official 'Senderos de Alicante' map, the PR59 (a variant of which we propose here) resembles a squashed stick insect, thin limbs poking out at odd angles and no very coherent logic apparent in the composition of the thing at all. On the

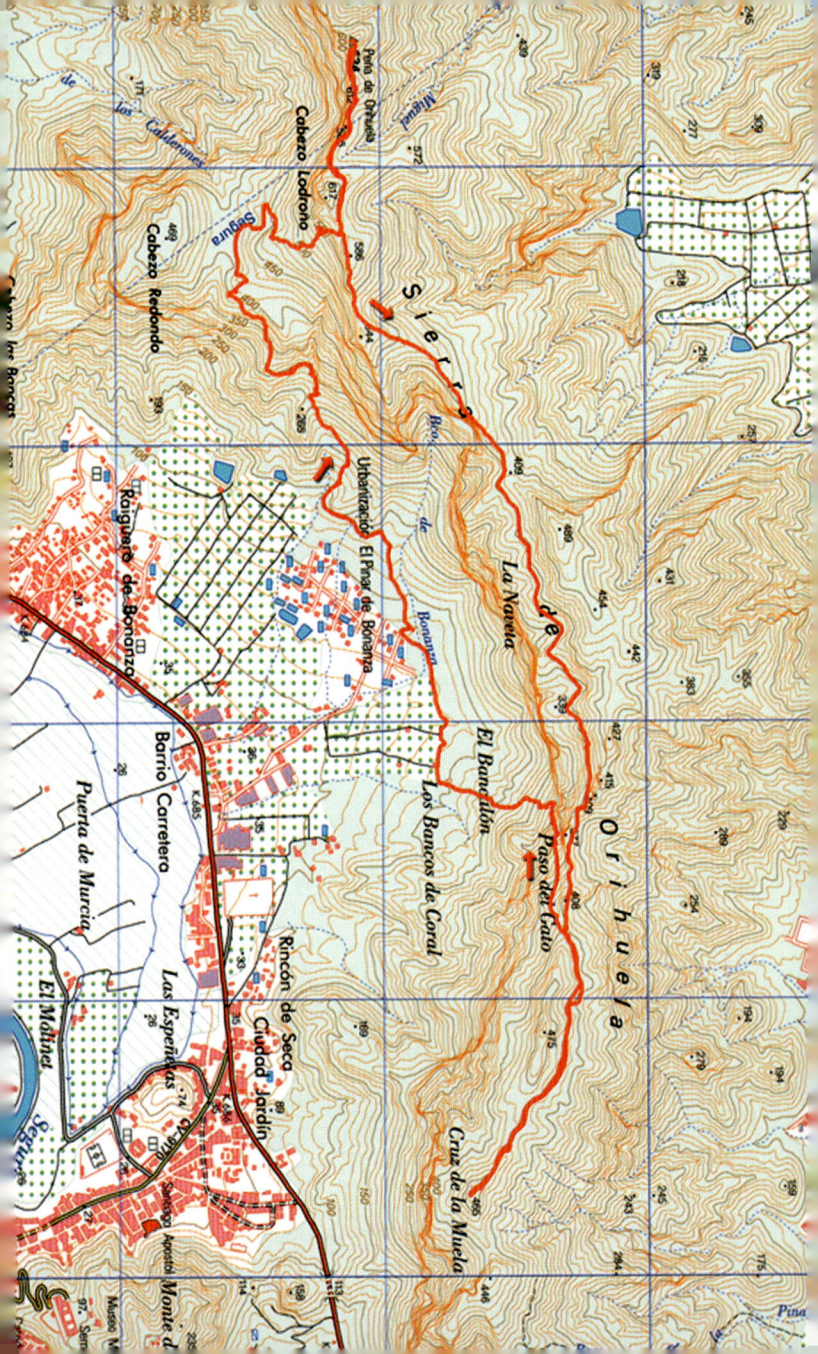

ground though, it's a splendid trail, so neatly waymarked, you're tempted to sit down and admire the directions as much as the views. Happily, the views are so very good, the more minute works of man are soon forgotten. As for the works of man on a larger scale, the plain looks considerably more appealing from above than it does when you're in the middle of it, the pattern of fields and roads and ribbons of development stretching away to the salt marshes and the sea like an elaborate plaid.

There's a slight risk of vertigo, but otherwise this is an easy itinerary that only gets its medium/difficult grade for one steep climb, some rough ground and a rather precipitous descent. The ridge is dry and exposed and not recommended in very hot weather.

ALTERNATIVE ACCESS:

Montepinar Urbanizacion on the Orihuela-Benferri Road

OTHER WALKS:

See the 50M, 52M, 2h, 2h16 & 2h30 junctions.

Getting to the Walk:

Just south of the 'Bar El Piste' at 'km.685' of the N340, take the turning between 'Chimeneas Martinez' and 'Ramon Transportes'. Fork left after 250 metres, turn right at 900 metres, then left 100 metres later, and park just below the chain at the end of the residential road, in front of a rusting 'Generalitat de Valencia' sign.

The Route:

Immediately beyond the chain there is a looped, asphalted track accessing the Rincon de Bonanza Area Recreativa. Follow the loop round to the right up to the *área recreativa*, just beyond which and a little above the tarmac track, a waymark indicates the start of the Sendero de San Cristobal, a good dirt path following a contour parallel to the track (7M).

After passing a junction with a path doubling back on the left to the bend of the tarmac loop (13M), the path starts climbing, zigzagging up to a small col beside a boulder with '1985' daubed on it (26M). The climb continues on a narrower but still clear path, crossing a gully and passing an arrowed 'Fuente' waymark indicating the San Cristobal spring (a few metres below the path and generally dry), beyond which are the ruins of a seventeenth century convent (31M).

Above the ruin, the path climbs more steeply amid a chaos of rubble, traversing a ragged slope of scree and debris to a shoulder overlooking Cabezo Redondo (42M). It then crosses a small pass and levels out, contouring round the end of the range, passing a junction with the 'Camino de las Yeseras' descending on the left (50M).

At the next junction, which lies a couple of zigzags to the north (52M), leave the main 'Boca del Puerto/Reguero de Levante' path and turn right for 'Cabezo Ladroño/Leja Millamon/Peña Orihuela'. The branch path climbs steadily to steeply, for the most part following a clear trail, but occasionally on more obscure ways crossing patches of waymarked rocks. This is the steepest climb of the walk, but it soon ends, quite abruptly at 'Punto III' of the PR59, a delightful picnic spot tucked under a couple of pine (1h10).

To visit the Peña Orihuela, the highest point of the sierra, climb over the spine of rock behind the picnic area and follow a narrow path along the northern flank of the mountain, skirting three small humps on the blade-like ridge, before scrambling up to the trig point on the summit (1h25). This diversion is purely for peak-baggers as it only marginally improves the views. Punto III is a perfect place for non-peak-baggers to while away the time while their companions play King-of-the-Castle.

Sierra de Orihuela

Back at Punto III (1h35), take the 'Cruz de la Muela' path to the northeast, crossing a small rise and skirting behind the hunched back of a precipitous escarpment. Traversing virtually pathless sheets of rock spattered with debris and waymarks, our itinerary descends to a Y-junction (2h), where we take the clearer, right hand fork, passing a variant doubling back to the left 50 metres later.

The path follows a contour below the rise of the crest, passing a succession of small caves and descending slightly to a second Y-junction (2h16), this time with the 'Paso del Gato' descent. Neither this descent or the next one are recommended on a first outing. Instead, fork left and follow the waymarks round the foot of the rugged pinnacles that have been visible throughout the descent so far. Down to the right, you will see a roofless ruin, which is where we eventually leave the waymarked route to return to the start.

Fork left again at the next Y-junction (2h30) and climb a shallow gully of quartz so friable it resembles crumbling sugarglass, passing onto the northern side of the ridge, where a clear path climbs to a junction with the path to 'Cruz de la Muela' and our descent via the 'Sendero Casa Forestal' (2h45). Once again, peak-baggers and breath-baggers diverge, the former forking left, the latter sitting down. Peak-baggers follow a nice shady path round to an open platform from where an alternative descent curves off toward the Urbanizacion de Montepinar and a broad trail leads to the Cruz de la Muela (3h).

The Sendero Casa Forestal (3h15) descends gently at first then more dramatically as it feeds into a long slanting ledge slicing across the face of the mountain. Despite the dizzying outlook and the constant impression that the way is about to drop into nowhere, the descent is never dangerous, however you do have to watch where you put your feet, as a fall would be no fun at all. After the junction with the 'Escalones/Paso del Gato' descents (3h30), an increasingly clear though occasionally skittery path zigzags down through the pine to the roofless ruin seen from above (3h45). Bear right here and follow a broad trail through the woods behind a couple of outlying houses back to the start.

Costa Blanca Walks — Sierra de Orihuela - 1

View from the top

2. Sierra de Callosa de Segura

Time: 2h15
Climb: 440 metres
Distance: 4.5km
Grade: difficult
Access: by car or on foot from Callosa de Segura
Short Version: La Plana

The Sierra de Callosa de Segura is like the obstreperous little brother of the Sierra de Orihuela, compensating for its more diminutive stature by being that much wilder and fractious. Take that as a warning. For some, this walk will be a definition of fun. For others it will be a nightmare. Given such strictures, you probably know already whether it's for you or not, but if you're still hesitating, let me emphasize that this is rough walking in wild terrain flanked by precipitous drops. There's a real risk of vertigo and the paths, though well waymarked, are sketchy at best. The walk is only recommended for experienced ramblers who take a positive pleasure from airy acrobatics. NB The rocks at the start can be very slippery with dew early in the morning. The walk is not recommended with a dog.

Alternative access:

a. Zona Recreativa Cueva Ahumada between kms4 & 5 of the CV900 between Callosa and Redován

b. San Carlos between kms692 & 693 of the N340

NB The stretch of the PR54 via Cox and the Castillo de Santa Barbara is a dreary drive and would be a deadly walk - avoid at all costs.

2 - Sierra de Callosa de Segura

Getting to the Walk

Just north of km6 of the CV900 in the centre of Callosa de Segura, take the westerly road signposted with knee high ads for 'Hiperoptica' and continue past the ELF station onto the 'Rambla Alta', passing a virgin on a pillar. Follow the road up through the Barrio del Pilar to the 'Pilarica Área Recreativa' and park below the chapel.

The Route

From the chapel, take the wooden footbridge over the main *rambla* (a dry watercourse), and bear left, passing a tapped spring and crossing an affluent *rambla*. Follow the PR-waymarks across bare rock onto the southern flank of a second affluent, where the path veers right and starts climbing steeply to the southwest (5M). Toward the top of the first climb, the path disappears amid steeply shelving sheets of rock (slippery when wet), but waymarks and a few crumbling cairns guide us onto a vertiginous ridge overlooking the CV900 and the verdant splash of a football pitch (15M).

Bear right and follow the waymarks along the ridge, favouring its southern flank (a real risk of vertigo here, but not dangerous so long as you keep your head - and your feet!), passing a steel cable set in the rock, after which a clear path leads to a small wooden bench facing Orihuela and Monte de San Miguel (25M). For the short version, continue along the PR until it ends, some 150 metres later, on the small spur of La Plana, then return via the same route.

For the full walk, leave the PR (ignore the yellow and white cross), and bear right (NW) toward the cabin you can see in the distance on top of the mountain. The path soon peters out, but pale green and dull red waymarks indicate the way forward. The route is invisible from below, but reasonably obvious each step of the way, and is confirmed by old waymarks every 10-15 metres. Following a series of faint ways and folds in the rock face, we climb to a slanting ledge marked with several cairns (35M). The steep climb continues across waymarked rock to a rough ridge overlooking the *área recreativa* (45M).

Care is required here as there are steep drops on either side and a nasty bit in the middle - downright horrible if you've made the mistake of taking a Pyrenean Mountain dog with you! Pick your way along the ridge (hands occasionally required) to a shallow col, where the ridge route is joined by the PR (55M).

Sierra de Callosa de Segura

We now follow the PR to the top then retrace our steps and use it to return to the start.

75-metres after the shallow col, the PR runs into a clear path. Fork right at a Y-junction with an other clear path (1h), initially squeezing through dense vegetation, then climb across waymarked rock into a steep declivity, from the top of which the principal Cox quarry is visible to the north (1h10). The remainder of the ascent is comparatively easy, climbing steadily to the southwest, past the cabin seen from below (a good refuge if required) to the Cruz de Enmedio (a.k.a. Alto del Aguila) trig point (1h20), where there's a spectacular bird's eye view of the Sierra de Orihuela and an absolutely horrible cliff - stay well back.

Retrace your steps to the shallow col at the junction of the ridge and PR routes (1h40) and fork left, sticking with the PR, which is rough and vertiginous, but less alarming than the ridge. The route, which is off-path almost till the end, winds down a succession of broad ledges along the northern flank of a narrow spit of rock, weaving through outcrops of rock and clumps of vegetation, passing another cable set in the rock (use it!) (1h50).

There are two ways down to the final descent. The PR bears right, across the narrow spit of rock, directly into a rubble strewn gully. We opted for the old green-and-red waymarked route, dropping down a steep declivity (hands and bottoms required) onto a shelf of rock at the tip of the narrow spit (2h), to the right of which a clear path descends alongs ide the gully.

Either way, once in the gully you can relax as the really vertiginous stuff is past, though some care is still required as the steep trodden way is slippery underfoot and progress remains painstaking. The path eventually crosses the silt dams behind the *área recreativa* and joins the track down to the chapel.

Costa Blanca Walks — Sierra de Callosa de Segura - 2

Precipitous drops abound

3 - Sierra de Crevillente

Sierra de Crevillente

3. Sierra de Crevillente

Time: 2h35
Climb: 450 metres
Distance: 9.25km
Grade: a slightly rough start, but otherwise easy
Access: by car
Stroll / Short Version: see text

From a distance, the Sierra de Crevillente looks a bit bland, a bleak, dry, monolithic lump of rock topped with a cluster of unappetizing antennae, but once you get into it, it's an extraordinary landscape of steep escarpments and fractured valleys endlessly interleaving with one another, the complexity of form compounded by the impact of natural erosion and strip mining. That proviso though, the one about 'once you get into it', is no small one, given that the one way system in Crevillente itself is so labyrinthine you begin to wonder whether they haven't got a couple of Minotaurs hanging about that they're anxious to keep tabs on. The way through town is perfectly indescribable, hence our rather roundabout route into the mountains, which may well be longer, but has the inestimable advantage of being intelligible.

The described route is a variant on the PR109 and also briefly coincides with the PR108, but this is one area in the province where you feel the waymarkers aren't ubiquitous. There are innumerable gullies, *barrancos*, *ramblas*, old trails and tracks, and unmarked paths waiting to be discovered and this is, more than ever, a 'gateway' walk on which you should keep your eyes peeled for alternative routes to explore at a later date. I suspect you could walk for a month in this sierra and find something new every day.

1 - Sierra de Orihuela — Costa Blanca Walks

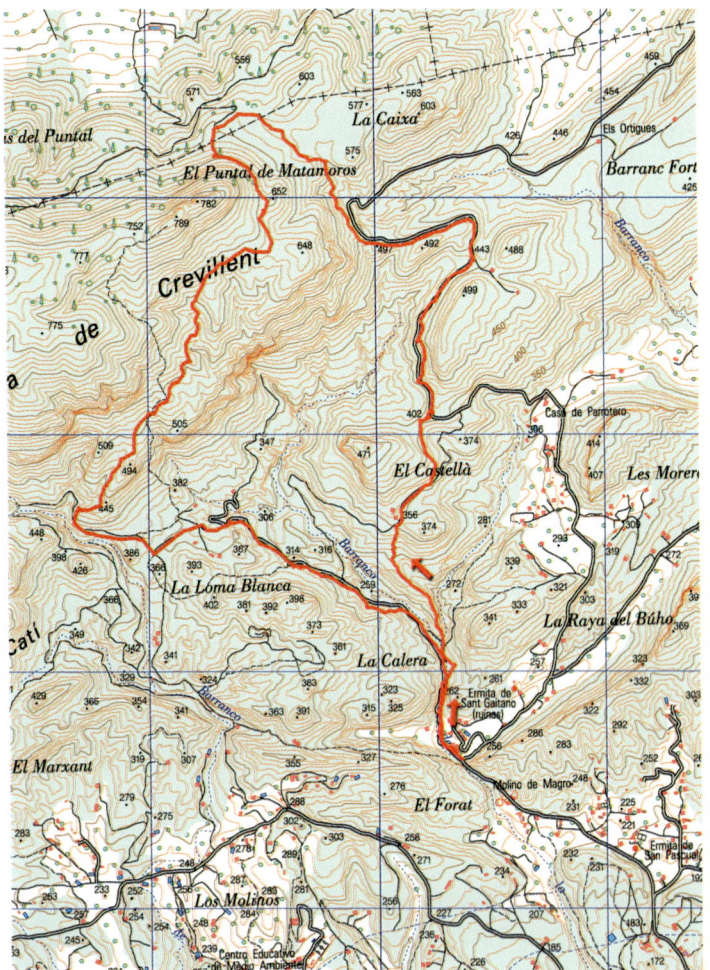

GETTING TO THE WALK

Take the N325 from the northern end of Crevillente toward Apse. Shortly after km18, 2.4 kilometres from the junction with the N340, turn left on the service road <u>behind</u> the Embalse de

Crevillente, setting the odometer at 0. Turn left at the T-junction at km1.8, then fork left at km3.7 and turn right at km3.9. Park at the Els Pontets aqueduct at km4.9 where there are mapboards for the PR108 'Sendero de la Serra de Crevillent' and PR109 'Sendero Dolça'.

OTHER WALKS IN THE AREA

    PR108   Sierra de Crevillente
    PR109   Senda Dolça
    PR110   Els Anouers
    PR280   Hondon de las Nieves to La Canalosa

THE ROUTE

Ignore the PR108, which follows the road under the aqueduct, and walk up the track into La Rambla, forking right into the riverbed after 400 metres for 'Barranc dels Corcons' (5M). Follow the *rambla* for a little under 200 metres then climb onto the spur at the confluence of watercourses.

After a steady climb, the PR meanders along the back of the spur amid terraces ravaged by erosion, then climbs a channel of rock, above which an obscure way dabbed with a couple of waymarks climbs directly across scrub patched rock to join a broad dirt trail below the white walls of an unfinished house and a well-preserved 'beehive' work hut (25M). For the stroll/ short version, turn left and follow the trail till it recrosses the *rambla* below the first house on the track, then take the track back to the start.

The PR bears right, passing below the beehive hut and following the broad trail for 225-metres before forking left on a minor path that climbs to a col and a well stabilized dirt track (40M). Turn left and follow this track to the north, ignoring a fork on the left 400 metres later, after which the track climbs

(NE) to an intersection (50M). Stay on the main, waymarked track to the left as it curves above the Barranco dels Corcons, at the head of which the PRs 108 and 109 merge, climbing to the left on a narrow path signposted 'Casa del Tío Mariano/El Raig' (1h).

The path climbs to a terraced swale with a few rather forlorn almond and olive trees dotted about. Fork right at a waymarked Y-junction (1h10) and cross better tended terraces until you reach a dirt track overlooking Hondon de las Nieves. Turn left then fork left 75-metres later on a rough track climbing past a ruin. We now leave the PRs, following a narrow trail climbing across terraces onto an abandoned dirt track, where we turn left, as indicated by an old mauve waymark (1h20).

The track climbs briefly then levels out along a contour before running into a narrow path (1h27) that takes us (SW) past a small cave fronted with a dry stone wall, after which the way splinters and becomes obscure. Follow the contour in a westerly direction and you'll soon find a clearer way marked by cairns, which leads to the top of a gully (1h35). Our path descends (SSW) along the flank of the gully then crosses a succession of watersheds and spurs before rejoining the PR108 (1h50) at a shady pine and a rough stone bench. Our itinerary now follows the PR back to the start.

Continue descending SSW, ignoring an alternative, cairn-marked descent on the left 75-metres later, and stay on the main path as it crisscrosses a long gully. At the bottom of the gully, turn left on a dirt track (2h05), then left again at the signposted crossroads 400 metres later (where the PRs 108 & 109 merge again) on a broad trail descending to rejoin the track used at the start of the walk. Follow the track back to Els Pontets.

Costa Blanca Walks — Sierra de Crevillente - 3

Along the escarpment in walk 4.

4. Two short walks in the Campo de Alicante

a. Sierra de las Aguilas

Time:	1h30
Climb:	250 metres
Distance:	4.5km
Grade:	easy
Access:	by car
Stroll:	the entire walk is barely more than a stroll, but if you want an even shorter stroll, turn left at the 20M point.

There are several enticing little lumps of rock rising abruptly out of the plain behind Alicante, but most are blighted by rubbish dumps or quarries, or are so inhospitable, even the Spaniards (a very robust people when confronted with a bit of rugged ground) haven't bothered beating a path up them. One of the rare exceptions is the Sierra de las Aguilas, which boasts its own immaculately maintained PR - the PR179 Ruta de San Pascual. In fact, it was a little too immaculate for my tastes, hence the present take on the itinerary, abandoning the waymarked path to climb to the summit of the sierra then going off path to get down again. Best done on a blustery winter's day.

OTHER WALKS IN THE AREA

There's plenty of scope for winter strolls following the tracks and paths round the foot of the mountain. The nearest PR (apart from the variants of the 179) is the PR169 at Aspe.

GETTING TO THE WALK

From Alicante, take the A31 Madrid motorway to reach Orito, a signposted exit less than 15 minutes from the A7. At the entrance to the village, turn right on a lane signposted 'Subida cueva', setting the odometer at zero. Fork right after 900 metres, left at km1.2 and park when the tarmac lane becomes a dirt track (km1.6).

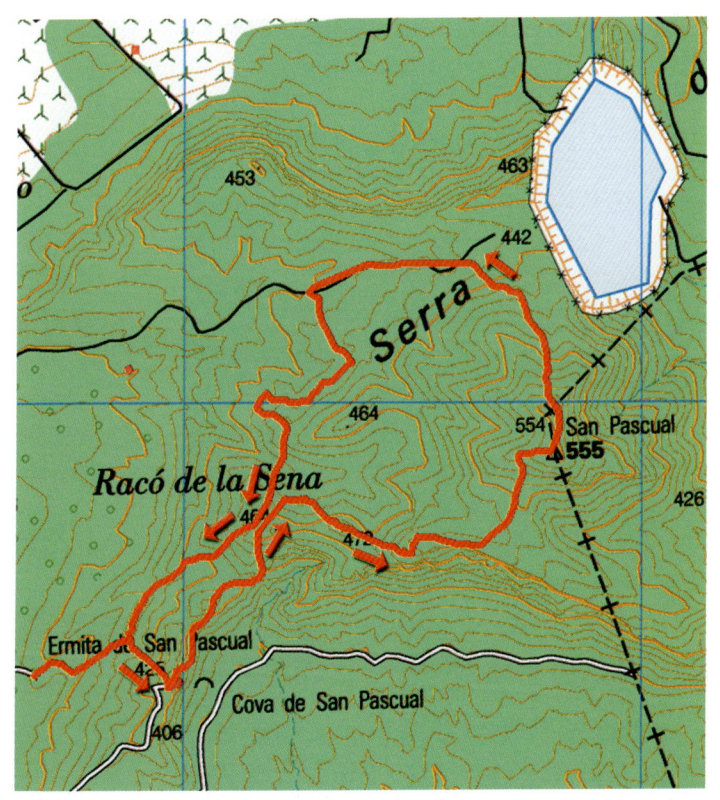

THE ROUTE

250 metres after the end of the tarmac, the dirt track divides at a Y-junction of trails. Take the branch on the right, briefly following a broad balustraded path, then climb across a long sheet of naturally stepped limestone to the shrine and cave dedicated to San Pascual, whose figure is sketched in stone on the slope below the shrine (10M).

Continue on the PR to the left of the shrine, passing a *mirador* before reaching a signposted crossroads (20M). Turn right, as if for the *'Sabina monumental'*, and climb to the next junction on a small rise 100 metres later. Rather than continuing on the PR, which descends directly, fork right on a clear but unmarked path leading to the escarpment on the southern flank of the mountain. Pass to the right of the first small crag, then fork left at the second (30M) and follow the path up to the San Pascual trig point, from where we have fine views of the sierras to the north (45M).

Continue along the brief ridge to the north, then descend (off-path but progress is easy in the sparse scrub) along the middle of three spurs fanning out toward a clear dirt track, heading for what appears to be a white metal tank - actually pale yellow concrete when you see it from close up.

Turn left at the concrete tank (1h) on the main track (the minor track immediately behind the tank soon peters out), rejoining the PR 350 metres later (1h05). Turn left on the obvious, wayposted path, then fork right 150 metres from the track to follow a serpentine path back to the crossroads near the cave (1h20). Turn right to rejoin the dirt track at the start of the walk.

La Murta

b. PR189 Barranco de Berlandi

Time:	1h25
Climb:	125 metres
Distance:	5.4 kilometres
Grade:	easy
Access:	on foot from Agost
Stroll:	turn left at the bottom of Parc El Rugló and follow the *barranco* to the Arabic bridge

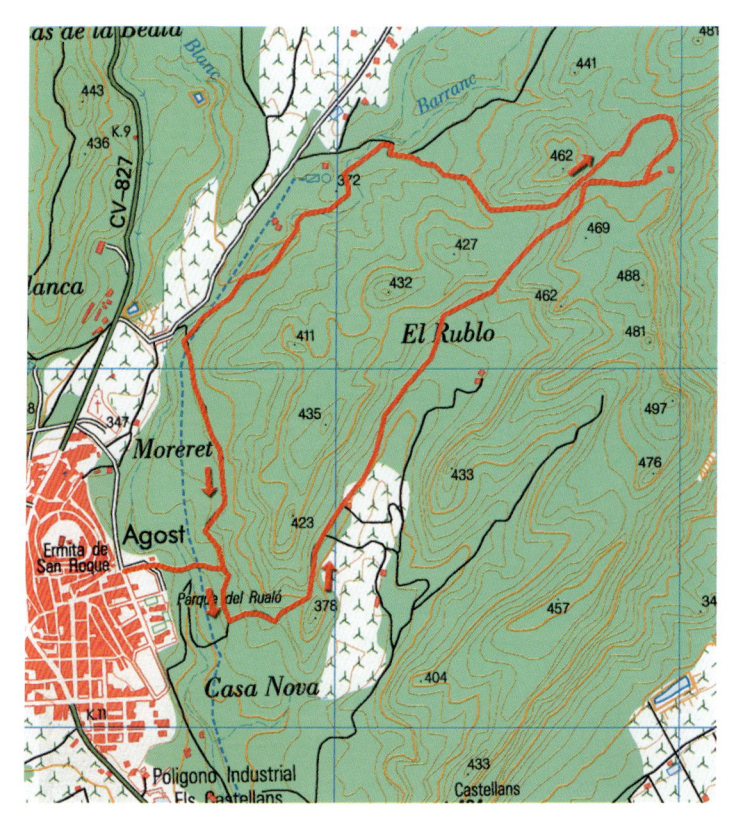

At first glance, Agost looks a little discouraging, its desiccated hinterland laid waste by drought and the ravages of the ceramics industry that still dominates the town. But like many of Spain's superficially devastated landscapes, once you take a step beyond the initial impression, there are some delightful corners, and there's endless potential for wandering aimlessly about the ancient paths, exploring the gullies, ravines and gorges that have resulted from centuries of use, abuse and the attrition of an inhospitable environment. You wouldn't want to be stuck outdoors here on a hot summer's day, but it's absolutely wonderful in Winter. Don't trouble yourself trying to find the Barranco de Berlandi on the military maps. It isn't there. Even on the official mapboard, it's the Barranc del Ventos.

OTHER WALKS IN THE AREA

    PR269   El Ventos

    PR274   La Creuta

GETTING TO THE WALK

From the centre of Agost (a 15 minute drive from the Alicante ring road via the A7 and the CV820) follow the CV827 for 'Castalla' to the city limits and turn right, following the brown signs to 'Parc Concepció/Rugló', where there's a mapboard of all three PRs. The PR269 leaves town further down the road, the PR274 200 metres back toward the CV827.

THE ROUTE

From the mapboard, descend past the recreation ground into Parc El Rugló and take the obvious steps climbing on the far side of the *barranco* to a dirt track, where a signpost indicates 'La Murta' off to the right (5M). Follow the track to the south for 250 metres, then turn left on a broad trail climbing to the right of a reservoir, from where a narrower, rougher path climbs to the northeast, joining an abandoned dirt track.

Bear left along the track, entering the Rollet valley, 100 metres into which, a signpost indicates the continuation of the PR, here dubbed 'Carrasca Centenara d'Agusti' (15M), on a narrow path along the western flank of the valley. At the head of the valley (30M), another signpost marks a path circling a shallow terraced basin to join a second abandoned track (35M). Turn right then immediately left and follow a stony way behind abandoned terraces to a pass overlooking the summit of La Murta, identified on the military map as Cerro Castellet (40M).

Agost

The PR descends here, curving round the far side of La Murta before returning via the same route, which all seems a bit futile, especially for a short walk. Rather than descending, I recommend bearing right (SSW) and following a faint way across the scrub, rejoining the dirt track at a signpost for the PR274. If you want to enjoy fine views over the Campo de Alicante and be sheltered from the prevailing winds, there's a nice spot 100 metres to the left, just beyond a locked, troglodytic cabin, known as the Casa de Tio Victoriano.

Otherwise, turn right and follow the track toward a scattering of outlying houses, passing a branch doubling back to the right, 25-metres after which a stubby waypost on a sharp bend marks a narrow path descending to the left into the *barranco* (55M). Follow the waymarked route as it crisscrosses the bed of the *barranco*, eventually joining a dirt track just east of the PR269 and the moorish bridge (1h10). Turn left and follow this track till it rejoins the outward route at the top of the steps above Parc El Rugló.

Immaculately tended countryside

5. Sierra del Cid

Time:	2h50
Climb:	550 metres
Distance:	9.25km
Grade:	medium to difficult
Access:	by car or (adding 5.4km rtn.) on foot from Petrer
Stroll:	600 metres after the alternative start, at the top of the first, 100-metre stretch of concrete, an attractive path off to the left descends to a small group of caves.

Whatever the truth behind the fanciful exploits attributed to Rodrigo Diaz del Vivar, the guy had sense enough to get a grand little mountain named after him, and if this wonderful walk is the nearest you get to the chivalric legends of Old Spain, you'll be as besotted as the man of La Mancha himself. The sierra is generally approached via the PR36 from Petrer, a route we use in part, but by far the most attractive path on the mountain is the dramatic Sendero de Contadero, featured in the PR6.6 from Rabosa. 'Contadero' paths are to be found all over Spain and are generally bottleneck routes herdsmen used to count their flocks as they descended from upland pasture. Certainly, no wayward sheep could slip past unnoticed on this fabulous path, which is of itself as improbable as any of the myths about El Cid, snaking down a cliff face that, when you glance back at it, is evidently impassable. There's a slight risk of vertigo here. The path is broad, well maintained and clearly waymarked, but traverses a steep slope above a cliff.

The ascent and descent are linked by a new dirt track, which is pleasant enough, but not hugely exciting, hence our rather out of

El Ginebre
La Madrona
Tadrova
Casa de l'Almadraba
Collado de Benissa
Clot Ventitos
Silla del Cid
Casa del Clot
El Xaparral
Trozo de Tora
Los Serranos

the way starting point. The Petrer access is far more direct and is the obvious starting point, but would involve ending the day on the dirt track. Begin at the eastern end of the sierra and the walk ends with the best bit. However, to accommodate those arriving from Petrer, we describe that access as an alternative starting point and detail the entire path, though there's a shortcut for those starting from the east to avoid descending all the way to the alternative start. There is an old path running parallel to the linking track, but this appears to have been abandoned and I suspect is cut by the new track, which is in any case OK at the start of the day. The track is drivable, but involves a very steep, clutch-blistering climb if approached from the western end.

GETTING TO THE WALK

First head for Agost, a 15 minute drive from the Alicante ring road via the A7 and the CV820. Follow the CV827 for Castalla to the city limits and turn left for 'Raco Bell', setting the odometer at 0. Turn right at the T-junction 400 metres later. Fork left at km1.6, right at km5 (100 metres after the bridge), left at km5.7, and carry straight on at the multiple junction at km6.9. Fork left at km7.1, carry straight on (the left hand fork) at km7.6, and turn right at km7.7. The Raco Bell *area recreativa/zona de acampada* (also known as Raco Xoli and Rincon Bello) is at km9.2.

From Raco Bell, follow the Petrer road for 1.5km then turn left on a well stabilized dirt track, which is surfaced with concrete after 300 metres. Park just after the concrete ends, 400 metres later. Note, this track maybe closed to traffic when there's a high risk of forest fire, but you probably won't want to be walking up here then anyway.

See Walk 6 for access to Raco Bell from Petrer.

ALTERNATIVE STARTING POINT

To reach the alternative start from the A31/N330, take the Petrer exit between kms34 and 35, on the eastern side of which is a Via Pecuaria and a mapboard for the PR36. Follow the PR waymarks along the Via Pecuaria (now a tarmac lane) for 2.7km, at which point a dirt track climbing to the left marks the alternative start of the walk, signposted 'Cumbre del Cid 1h30'. Park alongside the dirt track.

OTHER WALKS:

See Walk 6

THE ROUTE

From the end of the first stretch of concrete on the track climbing from Raco Bell, follow the track west for just over three kilometres (3.7km if you started from Petrer and this is the end of the walk), climbing 60 odd metres and descending 250. It's not the most exciting walking, but is a nice way to warm up at the start of the day, enjoying big views over immaculately tended countryside. There are two more stretches of concrete, the first 400 metres long, the second 100 metres. From the bottom of the 100-metre stretch, a slip path cuts up to the left to join the waymarked PR36 (50M).

Sierra del Cid

If you're arriving from Petrer, take the signposted path running parallel to the track, soon joining a narrower, abandoned track climbing to a terrace, which curves to the left, passing the slip path ten minutes from the 'Cumbre del Cid' signpost.

The trail zigzags up across crumbling terraces thinly planted with pine. There are numerous shortcuts, but it's best to stick to the waymarked traverses to avoid aggravating the natural erosion. After crossing a small rockslide pricked with mature oak (1h05), the path swings southwest to a final brace of zigzags onto a spur at the foot of the sierra's main southern bluff (1h20).The path continues climbing to the northeast, zigzagging up behind the bluffs on long traverses to a couple of cairns marking a minor fork off to the right (1h40). This is an alternative path along the top of the ridge, but serves no great purpose, so we stick with the better stabilized PR as it climbs steadily amid shrubby oak. Shortly after passing the half moon of a charcoal burning circle, the PR and alternative path merge for the final brief climb on a broad trail onto the Cumbre del Cid, marked by a large pile of stones. If you want to take a break, the best views are from the broad terraces just below the summit, overlooking some toe-tingling cliffs studded with climbing paraphernalia (1h55).

East of the summit, a rough, waymarked path descends steeply to join a narrow dirt track (2h05). Bear left and follow the track for 1.4 kilometres, bringing first the city then the *campo* of Alicante into view. Ignore the shortcut path after 1km (the views are better from the PR track) and turn sharp left 400 metres later onto the extraordinary Sendero de Contadero (2h30). The path soon coils down the escarpment, passing several mildly vertiginous stretches, though none so alarming as they look from above, before a long gentle traverse brings us back to the new dirt track.

6 - Sierra de Maigmo

Sierra de Maigmo as seen from the Sierra del Cid

6. Sierra de Maigmo

Time:	2h30
Climb:	450 metres
Distance:	10km
Grade:	medium to difficult
Access:	by car

Stroll: Take the track to the north behind the Raco Bell car park and follow the PR6.5 for Rabosa. Ignore a track forking right after 100 metres and bear left into the watercourse after 650 metres to follow a waymarked path climbing from a makeshift aqueduct. Stay on this path for a little under a kilometre until it climbs to a private house. Return the same way.

The PRs of Alicante Province are a very fine thing, ensuring that scores of classic itineraries are kept open and well maintained. However, it is possible to have too much of a good thing and occasionally one is seized by an urge to get off the beaten track and just make it up as you go along. As it happens, the PRs are so omnipresent and comprehensive, it's a job to avoid them without plunging into dense banks of gorse and plummeting off clifftops, and in this itinerary exploring the Sierra de Maigmo, we do use two PRs, the PR6.4 and 6.5.

Nonetheless, to turn two linear routes into a loop, we've trail-blazed a rough, virtually pathless ascent from the Raco Bell *área recreativa*, which is why an otherwise straightforward walk gets a medium-difficult grade. That said, the difficulties should not be exaggerated and, so long as you don't mind a little rough walking and are used to finding your way in mountains, this delightful itinerary should pose no problems.

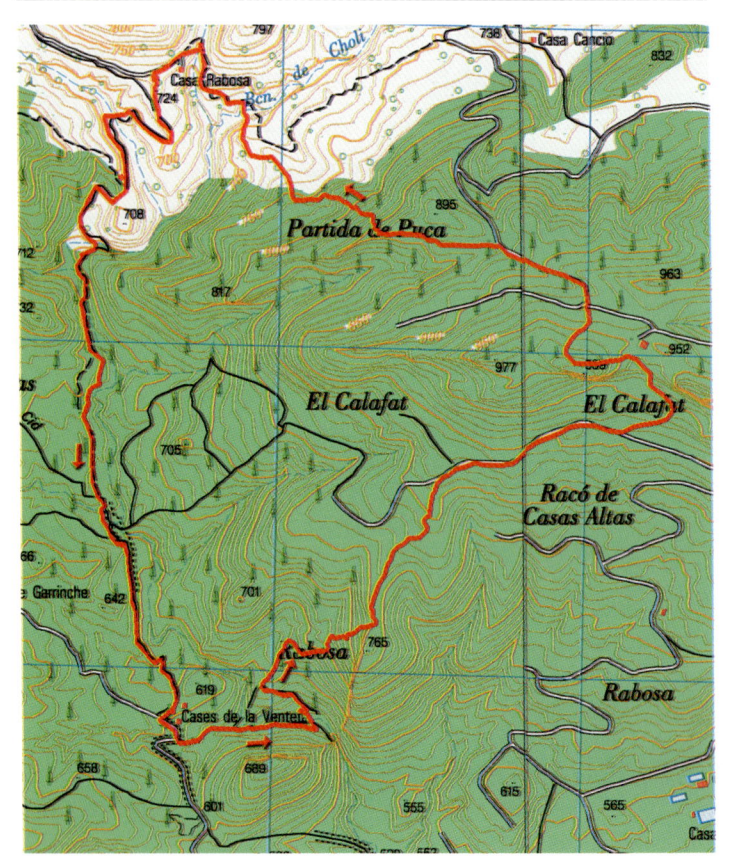

This is a 'gateway' walk and then some, as a glance at the list of other walks will immediately indicate, hence the inevitable glut of information before we get down to business. It's worth it, though. Both the Rabosa *área recreativa* and the Xorret de Catí estate are enchanting places amid great walking country.

GETTING TO THE WALK

See Walk 5 for access to Raco Bell *area recreativa/zona de acampada* from Agost.

OTHER WALKS AND ALTERNATIVE ACCESS

PR6.	1	Rabosa - Pinico Enfermo
PR6.	2	Rabosa - Castellerats - S. Bernardo
PR6.	3	Rabosa - Foradada
PR6.	7	Rabosa - Xorret de Catí
PR6.	8	Rabosa - Pantanet
PR6.	9	Elda - Rambla de los Molinos - Petrer
PR28		Xorret de Catí - Despeñador (Castalla)
PR29		Xorret de Catí - Alto de la Silla del Cid
PR30		Xorret de Catí - Rasos de Catí or Puça
PR31		Xorret de Catí - Alto de Guixop
PR32		Xorret de Catí - Cresteria del Frare
PR33		Xorret de Catí - Raco Xoli
PR34		Xorret de Catí - Pantanet
PR14	1	Xorret de Catí - Casa Tapéna (Castalla)
PR14	2	Xorret de Catí to the sea (San Joan)
PR14	3	Xorret de Catí - L'Avaiol

To reach Raco Bell from Petrer: take 'Carrer Sant Fransesc de Asis' then 'Avenguda Hispano America' up toward the castle. Cross the bridge over the A31 then turn left (signposted 'Raco Bell') setting the odometer at 0. Turn right after 150 metres and fork left at km3.1. At km6.7 the dirt track at the start of Walk 5 climbs to the right. The *área recreativa* is at km8.3.

To reach Rabosa and Xorret de Catí: from the commercial centres at the northern end of Petrer, take the Madrid direction access to the A31, forking left immediately after going under the bridge (you don't actually join the A31) onto the CV387, signposted 'Xorret de Catí'. The Rabosa road forks right at km

6.8, though it's usually chained after 1.5 kilometres except on Sundays and feast days. Xorret is a further 4.5km along the main road.

THE ROUTE

Before you set off, it's worth having a quick recce of the proposed itinerary. Immediately east of the *area recreativa* there are two sweeping curves of orange rock. Our route climbs across the terraces below the more northerly of these orange rocks to the tiny green dip dividing it from the next small grey outcrop of rock. The Lomas de Pusa (AKA Puça or de Catí) is the crest visible directly to the north.

From the Raco Bell parking area, follow the road down toward the lower part of the *area recreativa*, where a track, chained against access by vehicles, descends into the lower reaches of the *zona de acampada*, passing a refuge, shortly after which, we cross a wooden footbridge (10M). Take the steps across the first terrace, at the end of which a rough eroded track climbs to the northwest. After veering northeast, it dwindles to a trail, climbing amid young pine. The trail veers right again (ESE) onto the band of terraces seen from the car-park, where it more or less peters out (25M).

This is where the preliminary recce comes in handy. Keeping your eye on the green dip at the northern end of the orange rock, pick your way across the terraces, climbing steeply on a mixture of animal tracks and watershed channels. The dip feeds into a stony spur (40M) overlooking the Palomaret estate (passed en route if you arrived from Agost). Up to your left, you will see the next objective, some electricity pylons and a small transformer station.

Bear left (NNE) and follow a 'way' (off path but considerably easier than the ascent of the terraces) winding through oak

Loma de Pusa

scrub, aiming for the transformer tower. The tower briefly disappears from view, but favouring the higher ground when in doubt, you will soon emerge on a service road just below the transformer tower (50M). Ignore the fork to the left behind the tower and follow the main service road (ENE) up to its apex, where a rough dirt track climbs to the left (55M).

The track soon dwindles to a trail climbing to a large concrete reservoir on a col midway along the Lomas de Pusa (1h05), where we join the PR6.4. Turn left directly behind the reservoir, initially on the remains of a track, but soon following a narrow waymarked path climbing steadily to the second of the Lomas de Pusa summits and the end of the PR (1h10). Some care required here as there's a nasty drop on the far side of the crest. Continue in a westerly direction along the crest for 125 metres till you come to a Y-junction of paths (1h13), cairns framing the clearer right hand branch which descends through dense pine and oak scrub to rejoin the PR at a junction of dirt tracks (1h17).

Ignore the minor track turning sharp left (it looks more appealing but splinters into three forks, all of which peter out in the woods - I know, part of the penalty for making it up as you go along!) and follow the main track as it descends to the northwest. Leave the track 350 metres later, shortly after a stretch of concrete, and take the narrow, signposted path branching off a bend for 'Rabosa 2.8km' (1h21).

This fine path follows a contour along a spur dividing two *barrancos* then traverses a tapering band of rock before descending rapidly (a partially controlled skid is the best you can hope for if this descent isn't to take dark ages) on a stony path dropping off the northern side of the spur. The path briefly levels out on a terrace (1h35), after which a gentler descent leads down to the eroded *barranco* below the Rabosa *area recreativa*, which we reach via a neatly tailored path winding round an affluent gully (1h50).

The PR6.5 'Rincon Bello' starts in front of the large 'Centro Excursionista' building to the right of the triangular chapel and follows a dirt track winding along the complex folds of the valley to pass directly behind a private house (don't be put off by the 'Finca Privada' signs), where it dwindles to a path crossing a narrow watercourse (2h10).

Immediately after the watercourse, ignore a waymarked branch climbing to the right and stay on the path following the watercourse, passing an extraordinary little cave resembling a Cappadocian church, after which the path and watercourse briefly diverge. The woods here are criss-crossed by minor paths, so take care to follow the waymarks, which eventually return to the watercourse beside a makeshift aqueduct (2h20). Ignore the path that continues along the line of the interred pipe and bear left, following the watercourse to join a dirt track 50 metres later. Climb to the right then fork left at the signposted junction of the Rincon Bello/El Cid PRs, and follow the track back to the Raco Bell car-park.

Costa Blanca Walks — Sierra de Maigmo - 6

The off path start crosses the terraces on the right

View of the sierra from near the start

7. Penya Migjorn

Time:	2h35
Climb:	600 metres
Distance:	7.7 kilometres, nearer ten if you do the linear version
Grade:	medium or difficult depending whether you opt for the linear or looped version
Access:	by car or possibly (see below) on foot from Xixona

Xixona (Spanish Jijona) is the capital of *turrón* (a nougat-like sweetmeat that's *de rigueur* at Christmas) and nothing much else. However, there are some great walks in the surrounding mountains and none greater than this extraordinary loop encompassing the 'midday rock'. The views are exceptional, among the best in the province, and the main path to the top is easy. The full loop is not. Though not manifestly dangerous, it involves 500 metres off-path on a precipitous slope that won't be to everyone's taste. This might be best done as an ascent, but it seemed a pity that less doughty ramblers be deprived of the sitting-on-top-of-the-world sensation offered by the *penya*, hence this easy-up/tricky-down combination. Have a look, see what you think. If the described descent doesn't appeal, return by the same path. NOTE: though things were balmy enough when we visited the *penya*, the summit book is a catalogue of lamentations about the cold! Go prepared if there's a risk of wind in the Winter.

ALTERNATIVE ACCESS:

The PR212, which we follow throughout this itinerary, officially starts from the car-park at the southern end of Xixona, climbing to follow the Tibi road for 200 metres at km1.5 before joining the access lane described below. However, major works on the

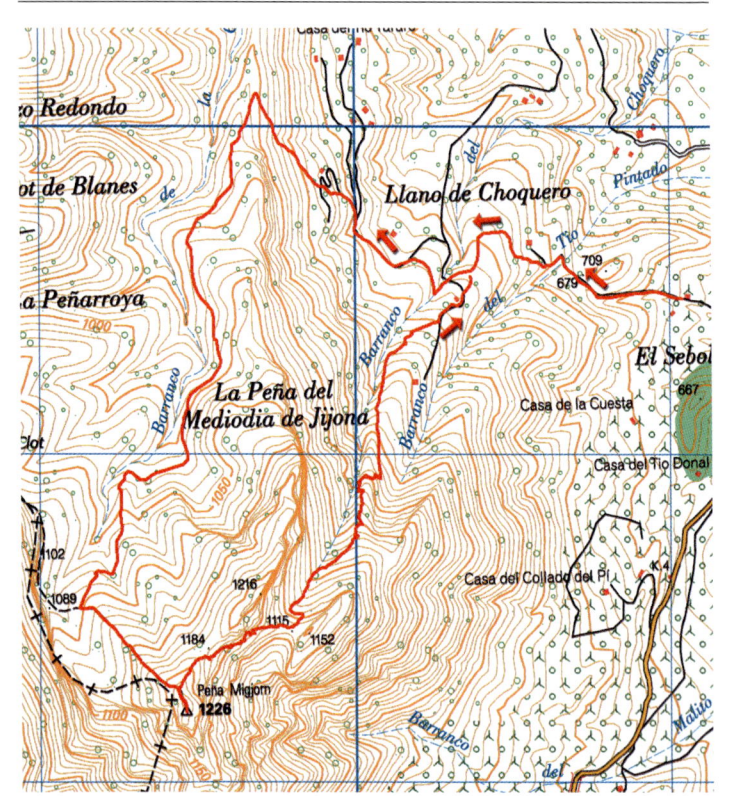

CV810 are making a mess of this at the time of writing, hence its exclusion from the present itinerary.

OTHER WALKS:

PR82	Ibi - Tibi
PR83	Ibi - Penya Migjorn - Tibi - Ibi
PR112	Xixona - Vivens
PR129	Xixona - Ibi
PR270	Xixona - Pou de Surdo

GETTING TO THE WALK

From the centre of Xixona, take the CV810 for Tibi and turn right on the 'Camino Rural' at the km2 milepost. Turn left 275 metres later and park at the end of the tarmac 400 metres after that. Parking is limited (2 or 3 cars maximum), so if the obvious places are taken, you may have to descend a little to find a spot.

THE ROUTE

From the end of the tarmac, follow its continuation as a dirt track for 500 metres, then fork left, maintaining a westerly direction on a signposted path (10M). The path climbs past a memorial cross, tracing a long northerly loop before veering south to a signposted junction (20M).

Fork right for 'Penya Migjorn per La Cova Corrals', crossing a dirt track 50 metres later to continue on a path that promptly veers right, joining a branch of the previous track. Follow this track up to the left, branching left at a triple fork. 50 metres later, fork left again on a narrow path climbing behind the house

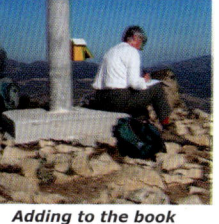

Adding to the book on the summit.

at the end of the track (30M). The path climbs (NW then SW) onto the eastern ridge of Barranco de la Cueva de los Corrales, where there's a signpost indicating a rather obscure link to the PR112 (45M).

Head south on a broad intermittently level trail leading to an attractive ruin at the terraced head of the *barranco*, the 'Cova els Corrals' (1h). The trail traverses a terrace then resumes climbing, dwindling to a narrow path before dipping down to one of the affluent watersheds feeding the *barranco*. It then climbs once again to reach another signposted link with the

PR112, in this instance one that follows a clear path (1h20). Turn left and climb steadily to reach the Penya Migjorn summit, the first of the obvious humps to the southeast, where there's a trig point, a summit book, and stunning views (1h35). Now for the tricky bit.

Seen from the Penya Migjorn, it looks like the onward path climbs onto the next pinnacle then promptly tips off the top. It's not quite as bad as that. Not quite. In fact, cairns in the crux between the two pinnacles frame a precipitous route, off-path but clearly waymarked, traversing the escarpment below the next pinnacle. It's invisible from the top, so you have to descend first to decide whether it's for you or not.

Retrace your steps to the signposted junction immediately below Penya Migjorn and take the 'Xixona 1h10' path down to the dip between the two pinnacles, where cairns mark the start of the traverse. Thereafter, follow the waymarks to the east, taking it one step at a time, heading all the while for the obvious pass above the patch of terracing to the south. Hands are helpful in places, possibly bottoms too, but so long as you take it easy and stick to the waymarked route, the danger is minimal. If, however, you suffer from vertigo or have two left feet, the linear route is recommended.

As the crow flies, the distance is less than 300 metres, but talk of crows and flight probably isn't very helpful in the circumstances. Actual distance is nearer 500 metres. In any case, allow 15 minutes to negotiate this delicate stretch, more if you're with someone who needs reassurance.

From the pass (1h55), a clear path zigzags down a broad shady valley (NE), then descends along the spur on its eastern flank, briefly crossing into the neighbouring valley before joining a stony track (2h20) 200 metres above the 20M junction.

Costa Blanca Walks   Penya Migjorn - 7

Not necessarily a barrel of laughs

8 - Sierra de Cabezón d'Oro or Cabeçó d'Or — Costa Blanca Walks

Approaching Raco de Seva

8. Sierra de Cabezón d'Oro or Cabeçó d'Or

Time:	3h30
Climb:	750 metres
Distance:	10.5km
Grade:	medium
Access:	by car

Cabezón d'Oro is the knobbly ridge visible from Campello and the N332 to the north of the provincial capital. It's a little less knobbly than it used to be since somebody had the bright idea of digging up the rock at its southern end and relocating it in Alicante, but the main mountain is intact and remains the most fabulous fun, great masses of rock (the official itinerary is subtitled 'Paisaje de Roca') bubbling out of the ground, eroded into ragged pillars and streaked grey with water stains. Framed by dramatic cliffs and dotted with delightful troglodytic refuges, it's the sort of place you could happily spend a whole weekend poring over, bivouacking in caves and underground dwellings, and gazing at the grandiose views across the greater part of the province's most celebrated sierras.

The PR2, which we follow throughout save for the spur onto the summit, is a well maintained trail, and more than adequately waymarked for the purposes of pathfinding, so once you've had a preliminary read through, you can safely put the book away. It does, however, have one significant drawback in that the official start either implies doing the main climb in the glare of the morning sun, or ending the walk with a steep 100-metre climb, neither of which are entirely desirable. To avoid this, we describe access to both the official start and an alternative way onto the trail that tackles the 100-metre climb at the start rather than the end. The walk is described from the alternative

Borralina
La Gorgonera
Mas la Gorgonera
Racó de la Mina
Partida de Cabeço
Casa Pla de la Gralla
Casa Gorjas
Mina Salvación
Mina Orcolana
Racó Seva
Mas de Racó Seba
Cabeço d'Or
Cabeço d'Or 1209
Serra del
la Gralla
CV-776
Cueva de Canalobre
de Bemat
Alto Salmitre
Salmitre
132 kV
Vidriet
Barranc
Umbria
Penc

start, but can easily be picked up at the official start. The path is immaculate, hence the 'medium' grade despite a hefty climb.

GETTING TO THE WALK

The official start: from Busot (accessible via the CV773 from Campello/Aigúes de Busot, or the CV774 Campello-Xixona road) follow the CV774 toward Xixona (signposted 'Cuevas de Canelobra') and take the CV776 for the *cuevas*, setting the odometer at 0. Park shortly after km2, where there's a small dirt parking area and a mapboard outlining the route.

Alternative start avoiding the climb at the end of the day: as per the official start, but at km1.7 of the CV774, take the lane heading north, sign-posted 'Pla de Cabeçó', setting the odometer at 0 as you leave the main road. The walk starts at km1.4, 150 metres after a small wooden house with a very steeply raked roof, on a signposted ('Coves de Canelobre') dirt track on the left. There's room to park at the end of the tarmac 75 metres later.

THE ROUTE

From the Pla de Cabeçó lane, follow the 'Coves de Canelobre' track (W) till it ends on a square platform (5M), above which a rough, rocky path climbs steeply, zigzagging up along the line of a narrow water-pipe, then traversing terraces (you can imagine what this is like at the end of the day) to reach the end of the CV776 and the Cuevas de Candelobra car-park (20M). Follow the road for 800 metres (look out for the spectacular perforated 'eye' in the rock up to your right), descending some

50 metres to a sharp left hand bend, where there's a mapboard marking the official start of the walk (30M).

Take the dirt track to the north, forking right after 300 metres to stay on the main waymarked track as it climbs along a stretch of asphalt. Follow this track for two kilometres as it curves round the mountain, passing an enviably located cabin (50M) before descending slightly toward the foot of a dramatic slice of rock resembling a wedge clumsily rammed into the ground. Turn right at the junction of tracks below the wedge (55M) and follow a narrower, stony track climbing in an easterly direction toward the abandoned Casa del Racó de Seva, ignoring a fork to the right 100 metres after the junction.

Directly in front of the Casa del Racó de Seva (1h03), leave the track and turn right on a narrow waymarked path, climbing onto and then traversing an abandoned terrace. The path zigzags up toward the main wall of the sierra, climbing steadily through easy loops, bringing into view the ivy clad mouth of a cave in the cliff to the south. The cave, which has a tailored entrance and a couple of sleeping ledges set in the wall, is accessible via a clear path cutting across a terrace behind a large solitary pine (1h20), and is well worth a 10-minute diversion, counted in subsequent timings.

After a couple more zigzags, the main path heads south, passing behind the cliff above the cave onto the flank of a broad, lightly wooded gully, at the head of which we come to a pass overlooking Alicante (1h50). To the right is a snow-gatherers' pit and the roofless ruin of the Casa del Polzet. 50 metres to the east, a second ruin conceals several interlinked underground chambers that make for a cozy shelter if required. Immediately to the left of the pass is the initially unmarked path (it features in some descriptions as part of the PR, but doesn't appear on the official mapboard) to the summit.

To climb to the summit, turn sharp left on the unmarked path that, initially, follows a contour through the pine (NE). The path soon starts climbing amid clumps of Holm oak, where older PR waymarks appear. After a steady climb, it runs along the bottom of a low cliff, which gradually tapers away in the approach to a two-metre slope of rock - hands required, and a bottom on the way back down, but nothing problematic and surmountable by dogs with a little light encouragement!

Thereafter a straightforward way winds through the rocks onto a col and climbs along the ridge to the north, passing a small roofless cabin within which there is another troglodytic refuge (this one housing an image of Saint Bartholomew, the patron saint of climbers) before reaching the trig point on the summit (2h15). Though we return via the same route, this is one summit that's worth the extra effort. The views are superb. Retrace your steps to the Casa del Polzet pass, taking care not to stray onto any of the precipitous, unofficial 'paths' more gung-ho ramblers have trail-blazed plunging off the side of the mountain.

Beyond the Casa del Polzet (2h30), the PR heads south toward the curve of Alicante bay, passing behind the eye of rock previously seen from the CV776, and descending across the Pla de la Gralla, a gently sloping plateau of scrub spotted with pine. After skirting a deep *barranco* at the southern end of the sierra (SSE), the path veers east for a while, but soon resumes a more southerly course (2h55), tracing out umpteen zigzags breached by occasional shortcuts. Eventually, 150 metres short of the power lines visible throughout most of the descent, it curves back into the *barranco* before joining a dirt track behind a house. Turn left to join the end of the road accessing the alternative start.

Acequia with Puig Campana in background

9. Cami de la Bacorera

Time:	2h15
Climb:	375 metres
Distance:	9km
Grade:	easy
Access:	on foot from Aigües de Busot
Strolls:	see text

One tactic when researching a book like this is to poke your nose in places no sane rambler would explore and see what crops up. Often as not, you uncover an unequivocally villainous spot or end the day clinging to a couple of dead weeds above a yawning chasm wondering whether there isn't an easier way to earn a living, but once in a while an oddity like the present itinerary pops up to compensate for the unpublishable experiments. In this instance, we explore the hinterland of Aigües de Busot, a former spa fallen on hard times that is only now beginning to rake in a bit of the lucre accruing from the tourism and expatriation that sustains so much of the coast. The walk is based on the PR243, an attractive path in its own right circling the Penyas Salmitre and Roja behind Aigües, but the novelty of our route is that we offer the option of following one of the *acequias* that striate the mountainside behind the defunct *balneario*.

Acequias are the ancient irrigation ditches pioneered by the Moors (or possibly the Romans) that are to be found all over the mountains of Spain and are still in use in many areas. The *acequia* we follow is of more recent origin and has long since been abandoned, but what it lacks in grace and vitality, it amply makes up for in the perfection of the walking, providing a mountainside pavement blessed with great views over Alicante and out to sea.

Ombría del Bacorero
Racó Ample
Cerro Salmitre
Pel Rotja
Salmitre
Casa del Racó Ample
Balneario de Busot
Foia de Coves
Pla de Perez
Casa de la Foia de Coves
La Caba
Balsa de la Caba
Casa de la Torreta
L'Altet
Altea
El Pino
Casa de la Palm
Caserío de las E
CV-7770
CV-775
757
675
801
619
667
674
494
586
585
564
397
421
411
412
445
444
490
463
498
451
383
750
700
650
600
550
500

The walk is exposed and, in hot weather, should only be done early in the morning or in the evening. Though the *acequia* is no longer in use, progress may be hampered by mud and puddles after heavy rain. The conventional start is described first for those who don't fancy the notion of a 'novelty' path or who are doing Stroll A, and it is on the basis of this version that the time, distance and climb are calculated. The main path is clearly waymarked and well maintained, and can be followed with only the most cursory consultation of the text. The main purpose of a description is to confirm that it's worth doing and pace progress.

OTHER WALKS
    PR226   Cami de Baranyes to Busot

GETTING TO THE WALK

From the traffic lights at km121 of the N332 just north of Campello, take the 'Aigües de Busot' turning to the North (turn right to cross the road via the half-moon roundabouts if approaching from Alicante), passing a turning to Busot after 6km. Park at the entrance to Aigües where there's a mapboard for the 'PR226 Cami de Baranyes'. Aigües can also be approached from Busot and via a minor road from Relleu, passing behind the Macaroba ridge and Los Barracones.

THE ROUTE

Conventional start and Stroll A:

Take the 'Relleu' road toward the 'Centro Urbano' then turn left immediately after the bus-stop and follow the slip-road as it curves round to the right to a mapboard for the PR243 'Cami de la Bacorera' (7M). Turn left and follow the tarmac lane, 'Carrer Bonavista', as it climbs toward the *balneario*. When the large ruined building of the *balneario* itself comes into view, fork right on a dirt track climbing in front of a large restored house fronted by two tall palm trees and a well (12M).

Turn right at the T-junction behind the *balneario* (18M) and follow the main track as it climbs past the water treatment plant to a col distinguished by a bright blue inspection hatch and a 'Coto Privado de Caza' sign, immediately to the left of which is the brick wall of the *acequia* (22M). For Stroll A, turn left here and follow the *acequia* to the south until you cross the deep indentation of a pronounced *barranco*, 300 metres after which a clear stretch of eroded land leads back down to the dirt track and the *balneario*.

For the full walk, continue on the main dirt track as it dips down and curves round a striking outcrop of rock off to the right fashioned like the shell of a vaulting turtle - a classic Costa Blanca land formation, a rising fault beached on a steep bed of opportunistic terraces. Directly behind the 'turtle', leave the main track, forking left then left again to join a narrow path neatly described by small stones that climbs to cross the *acequia* (33M).

Alternative start and Stroll B:

To reach this point via our 'novelty' path, take the *balneario* access road forking left from the entrance to the village, signposted 'Banys/Baños de Busot', setting the odometer at 0. Follow the road and the track it leads into curving behind the *balneario* ruin. Turn left at km1 and park at the third bench (km1.5). Follow the erosion scar up to the right for 100 metres then turn right on the *acequia* - and that is all you really need to know till you join the PR some 2 kilometres later. After 300 metres, the *acequia* winds into a pronounced *barranco*. At 800 metres, it briefly converges with the main track at the 22M point of the conventional walk (17M). Thereafter, overgrowth intermittently forces us off the *acequia*, which is partially covered for the next 400 metres, but easy alternatives lead along the terraces on either side. After crossing the remains of a dirt track and a narrow, slightly vertiginous bridge, follow the terrace alongside the *acequia*, now badly overgrown, to join the conventional route at the 33M point (35M). For Stroll B, turn right and follow the track back to the parking spot.

For the remainder of the full walk, take the continuation of the stone-lined path as it winds across scrub spotted with pine, bringing the main ridge of the Sierra de Cabezo d'Oro into view. After dipping into a swale at the head of a small gorge, the Barranc del Barber (50M), the climb steepens briefly, then slackens off for the last gentle haul up to a broad pass overlooking the Campo de Alicante (1h05). An attractive descent, only marginally impaired by the sheen of industrial greenhouses behind Alicante, zigzags down amid wonderfully pungent thyme to join a dirt track beside a deep fenced well (1h20).

Turn left and follow this track for a very moderate climb until it swings sharp left, at which point we maintain a southerly direction on a waymarked path (1h25). The path heads toward Alicante, initially on the level then snaking its way down across derelict terraces to join the end of an abandoned dirt track (1h35).

The track descends behind a breeze-block byre, after which it becomes broader and better stabilized. Turn left at the next two T-junctions (1h40 & 1h45) and climb across a small rise, ignoring a waymarked branch doubling back to the right (the PR226), immediately after which we pass the alternative start. If you opted for the conventional route, follow the track back to the *balneario* then double back to the right directly behind the ruin, returning to the start, initially on dirt track then on the old *balneario* access road.

Faro del Albir

10. El Faro del Albir & Punta Bombarda

Time:	1h40
Climb:	100 metres
Distance:	5.25km
Grade:	easy
Access:	by car or (adding 1.4km rtn.) on foot from Alfas del Pi
Stroll:	El Faro and back without descending to the mines

As a matter of egalitarian principle, I try to include in every guide at least one itinerary that would have your more gung-ho rambler rolling about the ground kicking his heels and displaying general signs of derision, and this is it, a gentle stroll along a paved way that would barely qualify as a walk at all were it not for the rough little circuit at the end and the lovely stretch of coast we visit. The stroll to the lighthouse is pushchair easy and I look forward to doing it again when I collect my Zimmer frame. The descent to the old ochre mines and Punta Bombarda is more arduous, but brevity robs the rough ground of any objective difficulty. Take a towel on a fine day with a calm sea.

OTHER WALKS

75 metres after the start, a paved way climbing to the right above the picnic area leads to the path up to the antennae on the summit of the Sierra Helada (see Walk 11), which is also accessible via the service road climbing from Castillo Compte d'Alfaz & Trinquet. The path climbing away from the picnic area splinters frequently, generally a mere divergence of shortcut and main route, but some of these alternative paths are attractive enough to be worth exploring in their own right.

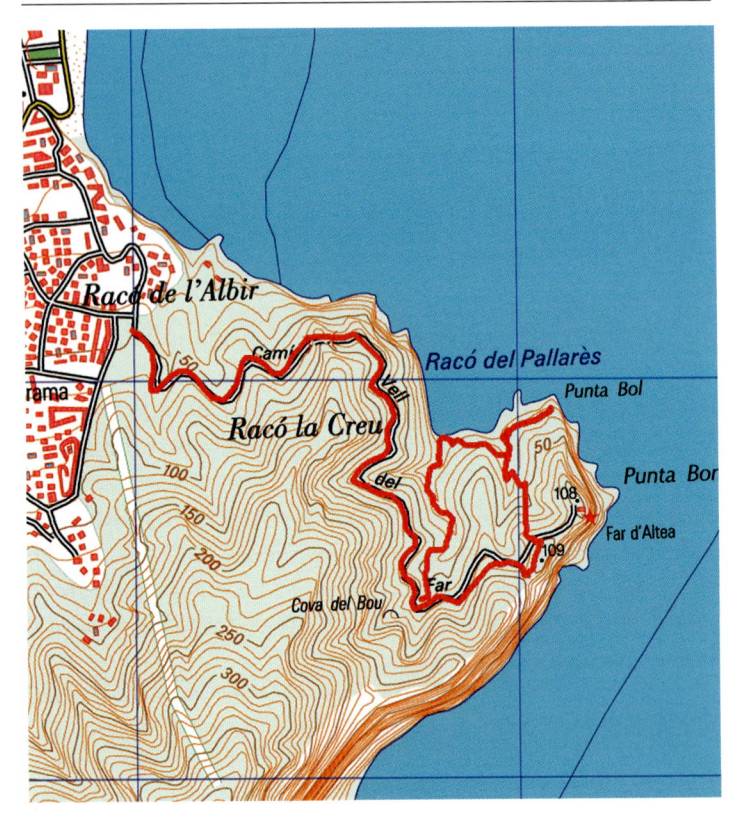

10 - El Faro del Albir & Punta Bombarda — Costa Blanca Walks

The regeneration programme for this sierra is on-going, so hopefully more routes will be cleaned up and waymarked in the coming years.

GETTING TO THE WALK

From the bus-stop/taxi rank in the centre of Alfas del Pi, take 'Cami de la Cantera' then immediately turn left on 'Carrer de Andromeda', which runs parallel to the high street. Follow it's continuation as 'Cami Vell del Far' up to the Carrer Neptu car-park, where a chain marks the start of the paved walkway to the lighthouse.

THE ROUTE

Simply follow the paved way for the 'Alfas del Pi Faro', enjoying fine views of the Bernia Ridge and the Penyal d'Ifac. After the km.1 milepost (15M), the trail snakes its way into a long valley topped by a deep overhang, La Boca de la Ballena or Whale's Mouth, below which two gullies descend to the sea. Ruddy stains of spoil below a pit mark the first of the ancient mines, originally exploited by the Phoenicians, while a tall post (25M) indicates a way up to the Whale's Mouth, which is now splashed with graffiti.

75 metres before the lighthouse gates (locked, but easily passed if you wish) (30M), a well-trodden way climbs to the right onto the ragged lip of dramatic cliffs and across a rocky rise, behind which it meets the fence around the lighthouse. Descend alongside the fence to the gate then continue alongside the fence, virtually off path and with a good deal of skidding about on the loose shale, down to the remains of the old mine works in the more easterly of the two gullies. From here, a clear path curves round onto Punta Bombarda (a.k.a. Bol) and a broad pleasantly isolated ledge overlooking a 20-metre drop into the sea (50M). NOTE: if you don't like the look of the unstable descent alongside the fence, steps lead onto an easier path below the point where we turned right to reach the cliffs.

Retrace your steps to the roofless ruins of the mine works, behind which a narrow way faintly marked with PR-stripes leads round to the next gully and a stony cove at its mouth (1h). Follow the waymarks up the gully, initially on the right bank (your left) then along the terraced bed of the gully, climbing amid dense vegetation (principally lavender, euphorbia, and pine scrub) to pass a small cave and the mine first seen from above, after which the outward route is rejoined just short of the Boca de la Ballena path (1h15).

11 - Sierra Helada

Sierra Helada

11. Sierra Helada (linear traverse)

Time:	2h20 (one-way)
Climb:	375 metres
Descent:	525 metres
Distance:	6.5km (one-way)
Grade:	medium
Access:	taxi and bus

Benidorm is bit like a new Rolling Stones album. Love it, loathe it or utterly unmoved, you probably already know what your reaction is going to be, and there's little point anyone else passing comment on the phenomenon, either to extol or belittle its relative merits. You might, however, be surprised to find a really wild walk on the city's doorstep, and yet the Sierra Helada ('frozen' as much for the aspect of its pale cliffs when seen from the sea on a moonlit night as for any climatic consideration) is as rough and rugged as anything in the region, despite the proximity of the tower blocks and burger bars. Don't underestimate this walk. It's tougher than it looks, requires stout walking shoes or at the very least proper walking sandals, and ought not to be tackled after a good lunch - the mistake that I made!

The route is relatively straightforward as we simply follow the crest all the way to the antennae topped summit, the Alt del Governador, but there's an absolute maze of alternative ways along the top. As a general guideline, the best path and the one most frequently waymarked lies between two and five metres behind the clifftop. The roller coaster effect of the rises along the ridge will put anyone familiar with the South Downs in mind of the Seven Sisters - only this being Spain, they added a couple more for good measure!

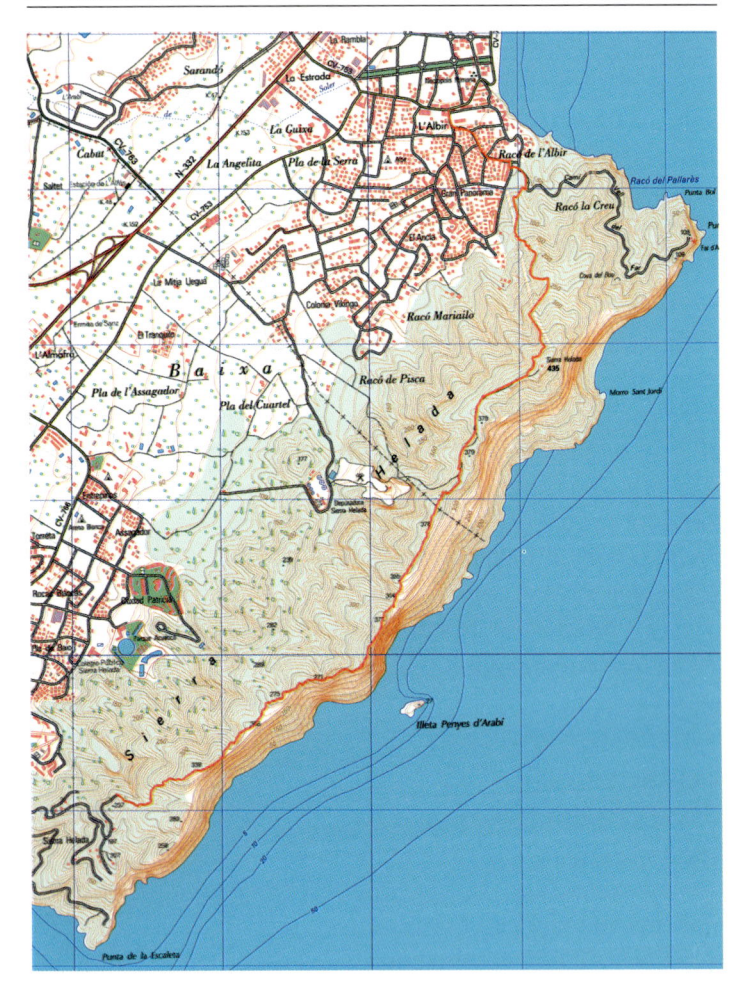

ALTERNATIVE ACCESS & OTHER WALKS

The ridge is also accessible from Rincon de Loix and from Aqualand. A pamphlet available in local tourist offices outlines the present itinerary and drivable strolls to Cala Ti Ximo and Punta de la Escaleta. Other options are mentioned in Walk 10.

Costa Blanca Walks   Sierra Helada - 11

GETTING TO THE WALK

The walk starts at the end of a separate itinerary in the Tourist Office pamphlet, but the route is demanding enough without adding this long stretch of road walking, so I recommend taking a taxi to the start. Ask for 'La Cruz' (the cross). If you want to walk the ridge both ways or have the option of going as a two car party (leaving one car in Alfas del Pi, see Walk 10 for access), set off from the northern end of Benidorm's seafront promenade, 'Avenguida Madrid', following the signs for 'Cala del Ximo/Sierra Gelarda'. Double back to the left at the junction with 'Calle del Alcalde Manuel Catalan' onto 'Calle Sierra Dorada' then to the right at the 'Edificio Dos Calas' sign. The walk starts 1.5 kilometres later, at the end of the road.

THE ROUTE

At the end of the road, three paths fork into the sierra. Take the lower, left hand forks at the first two junctions in the first 50 metres, following faint PR waymarks and, rather more usefully, ancient ruddy dots and ruby red arrows. A steady climb on bare rock leads to the second of the two rises behind La Cruz (20M). These clifftop rises are the best way of pacing progress, so if you care to compare your times with mine, start counting.

The path subsequently drops down steeply to a densely wooded col (30M) overlooking Isla Mitjana, also known as Peñas de Arabí, the redoubt of gulls, including the rare (otherwise only found in the Balearics and the Eastern Mediterranean) Audouin's Gull. A marginally less steep climb crosses rises 2 and 3, before we again descend steeply from No.4. NB Take care not to stray onto the cairn-marked path descending inland from rise No.3.

At the bottom of the second steep descent, we pass a concrete lined pit (45M), after which a steady climb leads to the stump of a ruined cabin (55M). Rise No.5 is a long blade like affair (peer over the cliffs and you'll see just how cutting it can be... on second thoughts, don't!) ending, you've guessed it, with a third steep descent. Rise No.6, though relatively brief, provides the stiffest climb yet. A very moderate descent precedes rise No.7, after which you can breathe easy as the next three rises can be avoided by descending directly to the Alt del Governador service road (1h30).

A gentle stroll along the asphalt comes as quite a relief after the rough paths on the rest of the ridge. Passing a couple of fields and a water reservoir, the road climbs steadily toward the antennae, 50 metres before which a large cairn and a red dot mark the path descending to Alfas del Pi (1h40).

This path, which is a lot less rough and stony than the main traverse, dips through a tiny chicane before descending to a spur lined with electricity pylons. Ignore the shortcuts and follow the main, knee-preserving traverses as they descend into a pine wood, where tighter turns zigzag down a gully before emerging at the head of a *dehesa* (partially cleared woodland) and a crossroads of paths marked by a large cairn (1h55). Turn left here on a broad dirt trail, descending through the *dehesa* to converge once more with the pylons. Follow the pylons down to a clear way lined and, in the last few metres, paved with stone, which descends on the right to the picnic area on the Faro del Albir trail (see Walk 10).

Turn left then cross the Carrer del Neptu car-park and follow Carrer del Neptu and Carrer Siria down to the centre of Alfas del Pi, reaching the high street in front of the taxi rank and bus-stop. Buses back to Benidorm are hourly until around 10 pm.

Isla Mitjana

12 - Puig Campana   Costa Blanca Walks

The central gully used in the ascent

12. Puig Campana

Time:	4h05
Climb:	1150 metres
Distance:	10 kilometres
Grade:	difficult
Access:	by car or (adding 2km rtn.) on foot from Finestrat

There's no way round it. When it comes to Costa Blanca walking, Puig Campana is The One. Towering over everything else near the coast, its soaring dome fluted with turrets, towers and fanciful crenellations, it would be all to easy to conclude this dramatic summit was the model for Gaudi's famous expiatory temple, the Sagrada Familia. Moreover, the coastal association is indisputable. Just as the northern rock of the Penyal d'Ifac and the southern Rock of Gibraltar were landmarks for Phoenician navigators and the Sierra Helada is 'frozen' for the white aspect of its moonlit cliffs, Puig Campana was a mariners' mountain, the village of Finestrat getting its name from the '*finestra*' or window of the Tajo de Roldan (AKA El Portell), the notch that is the summit's defining feature when viewed from the sea.

The ascent looks daunting from a distance (from the south it's the long grey green scar in the middle of the mountain - yes, *that* one!) and it can get pretty daunting on the ground, too, but there are no technical difficulties, no marked danger, and the walk only gets a difficult grade for the steep climb. Otherwise, it should pose no problem for anyone who is reasonably fit or used to putting their body through a few punishing paces. Still, it's worth remembering the Spanish maxim, "*Con calmo y tranquilidad, todo se hace*" - with calm and tranquillity, everything is doable (I translate freely). Take it easy and go prepared for a full day's outing.

Collado del Povet
882
A
B
El Maset
Mas del Oficial
Dalt
743
1087
Sierra
La
Mas Pintat
de Geroni
1249
Puig Campana
1408
1406
Puig Campana
Racó del Gatet
1344
1318
803
d'Albardalet
1065
Cova del Roget
Racó de les Nou Houres
664
Racó de les Nou Hores
543
412
Puerto
Foia del Cap
528
Costera Blanca
506
Casas del Ramal de l'oix
Font del Moll
416
L'Alhambra
323
Almacil
Font de l'Alquería
342
L'Alquería
Salt
Antons
CV-758
Casas de Raval
Finestrat
Casa del Tamarit
Arenetes
Tapiada
Ermita Cristo del Remedio
266
CV-761
Els Marjalets

In theory, we follow the PR14 for the ascent, 'in theory' because it soon becomes clear that once the going got tough, the waymarker got weary and made a discreet withdrawal - you can understand the sentiment. In the maze of ways approaching the main ascent, we follow the PR waymarks. Thereafter, we rely on older red dots and arrows. The route is not recommended in reverse as the gruelling ascent would make a very painstaking descent.

NB Two months after this walk was recorded, a forest fire laid waste the woods on the western flank of Puig Campana. Not all the trees are dead, so there is some hope of a partial recovery, and cistus will inevitably do its usual job of greening the mountain. Nonetheless, it's worth driving a little further up the road to see what state it's in before doing the walk. If it still looks grim, do the alternative return via the *solana*.

OTHER WALKS

PR12   Finestrat - Sella
       (better done as a cycle ride than a walk)

PR13   Finestrat - Polop

The following paths and tracks are outlined in a pamphlet available from the Tourist Information Office in Cala de Finestrat:

Cami de la Cala

Cami Vell de Polop

Cami Vell d'Alacant

Cami Vell d'Alcoi

Cami de la Cova de Roget

ALTERNATIVE SHORT WALK: Sierra Cortina

Timing:	1h (rtn.)
Climb:	220 metres
Distance:	2.6km (rtn.)
Grade:	easy
Access:	by car or bus

The Sierra Cortina (the 'curtain' I guess to the 'window' of the Tajo de Roldan) is a long low rocky hill lying between Puig Campana and the coast. It's nothing extraordinary, but there's a well waymarked linear traverse which makes for an agreeable short walk when the weather discourages an ascent of the Puig itself.

To reach the start, take the CV70 from Benidorm toward Callosa and follow the 'Terra Natura' signs to car-park 1, accessible by buses 21 & 22. From the bus stop, continue along the road (on foot or by car) for 500 metres then turn right at the roundabout. The path starts on the left of the road 400 metres later, where there's a signpost visible from the road and, just out of sight, a mapboard. Motorists will have to continue on the Finestrat road (the CV758) for another 100 metres to park in the lay-by on the left of the road.

As I say, the walk is well waymarked (red and white GR-style stripes), so description is redundant. Suffice to say the path drops into the gully alongside the access road, then climbs to join a dirt track just short of the wooden superstructure of the first *mirador*. 50 metres later, a wayposted path climbs to the left to follow a circuitous but clearly waymarked route climbing to the second *mirador*, which is framed by two trig-points. Return the same way.

GETTING TO THE MAIN WALK

From the centre of Finestrat, follow the brown signs for 'Font del Molí' and park in the *área recreativa* car-park just after the *fuente*. One can also park at the bridge 350 metres later, where the walk leaves the road, but space is more limited.

THE ROUTE

Continue along the road above the car-park for 350 metres, ignoring a waymarked track on the right (the PR289), then fork right, leaving the road just after a bridge over a concrete canal (10M). Follow the signposted route of the 'PR14 Puig Campana', a broad trail climbing through pine woods. Fork right at a Y-junction 200 metres later to climb more steadily on a narrower trail, looking out for PR-waymarks when the trail disappears in sheets of rock or diverges from other waymarked routes.

The trail dwindles to a path alongside the Barranco de las Marietas, climbing amid a rockscape that give every impression the mountain has recently stopped melting. At the head of the *barranco* proper, the path levels out briefly (30M) and veers left (N) before resuming its steady climb alongside the terraces at the foot of the steep, stony watershed used for the main ascent.

The path soon becomes confused, confused enough to lose the PR waymarker, but progress is straightforward. Simply stay on the left bank (our right) of the terracing/watershed, and look for the red waymarks when in doubt.

The way eventually passes below a low wall of rock (spattered with graffiti immortalizing 'Ana' and an assortment of local lasses who've stimulated the ardor of Alicante's outward bound adolescents) (1h), apparently within spitting distance of the top. Don't spit yet, though. The toughest bit is still to come. Remember, *con calmo y tranquilidad*. Stay on the eastern side of the watershed and follow the waymarks (except for one large red dot on the western flank, which marks an altogether more life threatening ascent), climbing steeply but not as steeply as it looks from below - or, for that matter, above. Much of the way traverses unstable debris and loose gravel (you can imagine what it would be like coming down on this stuff), but there are some vaguely path-like patches of dirt skirting the worst of the rockslide.

Eventually (and it's a big 'eventually'), hopefully with all members of your party still enjoying *calmo y tranquilidad*, cairns mark several ways over larger debris onto the broad pass known as the Bancal del Morro (1h55), from the northern edge of which, superb views open out over the Sanxet and Ponoig summits and, beyond, the Sierra de Aixorta.

To reach the top, take any of the paths climbing to the right - the blue waymarked route is easiest underfoot. The path passes a small weather station, then curves round the eastern flank of the summit before a brief final climb leads to the trig point (2h15). After you've enjoyed the stunning views, follow the obvious path back to the southwest to make a short loop, then retrace your steps to the Bancal del Morro (2h30).

From the northern end of the pass, a clear path descends toward Sanxet and Monte Ponoig, weaving between Holm oak and pine. After the arduous ascent, this good dirt path with only a scattering of loose stones, looks like a doddle, but it's still spectacular. The gradient steepens, dropping down through a series of giddying twists and turns, some so tight they resemble a concertina. After traversing a rockslide (2h50), the path descends through denser more mixed woodland, broadening to a trail then a track, which leads to a junction with the PR289 (3h). This is where you must decide which route you take back to Font del Moli. Both are well-waymarked, so once you've glanced through the outline, stow the book.

a. Via the western flank: fork left, staying on the track, then turn left at a major intersection on Coll de Pouet to follow 'Cami de la Serra'. The track dwindles to a path above a metal refuge dedicated to 'José M. Vera' (3h10), beyond which a clear path squirms along the fire-damaged flank of the mountain. It eventually bears away from the main rise of rock, diverting onto the El Volador spur (3h35). After a brief but steady descent, the path follows a long contour, then drops down to a Y-junction (3h50). Fork left and descend to cross a dirt track, rejoining the outward route at the road 300 metres later.

b. Via the *solana*: turn right and follow the waymarked path (ESE), passing a signpost for Font del Moli after 300 metres. The path then curves south, descending across a rocky hillside on which it passes a deep sinkhole. 750 metres later, the PR enters woodland, passing a red waymarked path branching off to the left. After twice crossing the 'Refugio Pedre de Tio Frare' dirt track, it descends through woodland to join another, better surfaced track. Turn right and follow this track back to the *area recreativa*.

13 - Barrancos del Arc & Charquer — Costa Blanca Walks

Daunting for some delightful for others

13. Barrancos del Arc & Charquer

Time:	3h40
Climb:	570 metres
Distance:	13.3km
Grade:	medium
Access:	by car or (adding 8km rtn.) on foot from Sella
Stroll:	Barranco del Arc (linear)

The mountains near Sella are popular with climbers, understandably when you see the cliffs, a glance at which is enough to cue cold sweats and a curling of the toes in timorous souls like me. But there's more (or less, depending on your point of view) than eye popping audacity to these mountains, and some of the PRs are possibly a little too tame, sticking to perfectly drivable dirt tracks. In this itinerary, we make use of three PRs, linking the two featured *barrancos* by a little known goat track traversing the Loma de Serventa. There's one steep, rough climb in the middle, but otherwise it's all easy walking with great views. Best done on a weekday as the dirt tracks can be busy with local traffic at the weekend.

OTHER WALKS

PR9	Sella to Benimantell (see text)
PR10	Sella to Benifato
PR11	Tafarmatx (see text)
PR12	Sella - Finestrat (see text)

GETTING TO THE WALK

From the eastern entrance to Sella, take the lane to the northeast, signposted 'Barranc de l'Arc/Font de l'Alcàntara'. Follow this lane (which coincides with start of the PRs9, 11 & 12) for a

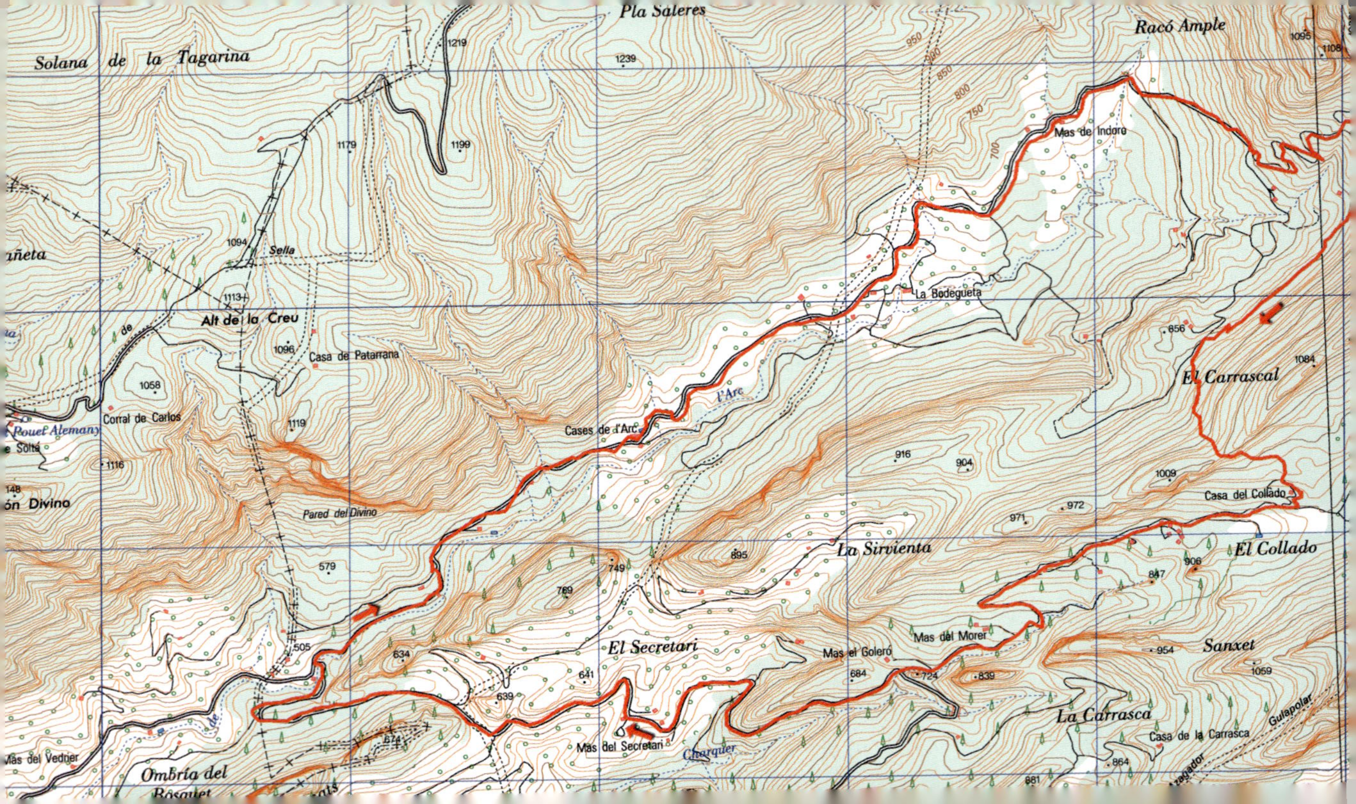

Pla Saleres
Solana de la Tagarina
Racó Ample
Mas de Indoro
Sella
Alt de la Creu
Casa de Patarrana
Corral de Carlos
Pouet Alemany
Pared del Divino
Cases de l'Arc
l'Arc
La Bodegueta
El Carrascal
Casa del Collado
El Collado
La Sirvienta
El Secretari
Mas del Secretari
Charquer
Mas el Goleró
Mas del Morer
Sanxet
La Carrasca
Casa de la Carrasca
Gulapolar
Mas del Vedner
Ombría del

little over four kilometres until the end of the tarmac. Park on the eastern flank of the valley, behind the climbers' refuge.

THE ROUTE

From the parking area behind the refuge, return to the end of the tarmac and take the continuation of the PR9 up the valley for 'Benimantell'. The track climbs gently amid young pine, poplar, oleander, carob and strawberry trees, backed by attractive escarpments streaked with water stains, soon passing several of the mountain *cortijos* that characterize this route, notably (the third and largest of the early farms) L'Arc de Canonge (30M).

Stick to the main track as it climbs into the broad basin at the head of the valley, where it levels out, passing behind 'La Bodegua', presumably a reference to viniculture rather than the establishment's status as a dispenser of alcoholic beverages. Fork right a couple of minutes later at the rusting, waymarked carcass of a small car, then left almost immediately (50M).

The track resumes its ascent, passing a small goat farm with a corral built into cliffs behind the farm. Fork left at the major Y-junction a few hundred metres later (1h10), where the first steady climb begins, passing a gated track (sporting a pair of puzzling plaques the same colour as PR waymarks) (1h20) that leads to a large grey *cortijo* directly to the south. We pass this *cortijo* later, but for the present, stay on the main track as it continues climbing, zigzagging up toward the pass into the Guadalest valley.

100 metres below the pass, at a sharp left-hand bend just before a decrepit black-and-white sign, turn right on a narrow path marked with cairns (1h35). The path (which is soon picked out with old red waymarks) descends (S), toward the grey *cortijo*, joining a broader trail between the main building and

13 - Barrancos del Arc & Charquer — Costa Blanca Walks

a diminutive cabin (1h40). Follow this trail to the southwest, traversing terraces that have clearly been damaged by fire in the distant past, and are now swathed in cistus and oak scrub.

When the trail joins the dirt track running behind the house (1h50), maintain direction on the track for 200 metres until you see a large red waymark indicating an otherwise invisible path climbing through the scrub to the left (1h54). Once you're on it, the path (which is little more than a waymarked goat track) is reasonably clear, but the waymarks are useful confirmations that you're still on trail as you climb steeply (S) on a rough, slippery, stony way. Toward the top, the oak become increasingly dense, but the way is never wholly obscured and soon emerges on top of the ridge (2h10), from where superb views open out to the east.

Ten metres to the left, a natural pass leads onto our way down, a much clearer and better graded path descending into the pine. After skirting a bend in a minor track, the path traverses a terrace and joins the end of another minor track at a satellite cottage behind Mas El Collado, a large, beautifully rebuilt farmhouse that was visible from the ridge (2h17).

Follow this track as it descends to the right, feeding into the PR15 (see Walk 16) and passing some delightful cabins and cottages. The track passes the 'El Morer' Buddhist retreat (2h40), then joins another track at a bend and, 150 metres later, the main Sella to Finestrat dirt track (the PR12) (2h50). Description is perfectly redundant hereafter, as we simply bear right and follow this track as it curls around the Barranco del Charquer before passing the Mas de Moelen and descending behind the main Sella climbing walls back to the starting point in the Barranco del Arc.

Barranco del Arc

14 - PR.198 Alto de la Penya de Sella — Costa Blanca Walks

Puig Campana seen from the descent

14. PR198 Alto de la Penya de Sella

Time:	3h30
Climb:	700 metres
Distance:	9.5km
Grade:	very difficult
Access:	on foot from Sella
Stroll:	see alternative access

This walk shouldn't really be a PR at all. It's an off-path scramble, not a walk, featuring an incredibly tough climb amid a landscape so wild it's a wonder anyone volunteered to visit it with a couple of pots of paint in their rucksack in the first place. In fact, they seem to have had second thoughts, as the waymarks stop halfway round, leaving the hapless rambler (me, for example; I had to go back the next day to find a descent that was at once desirable, describable and safe) floundering about looking for a non-fatal way off the cliff's edge. The problem is threefold: first, there's no clear path; second, most waymarks have been done for people coming up; third, someone has gone round diligently defacing all the readily accessible waymarks on the ridge! Moreover, even on the ascent, which is well waymarked, excellent pathfinding skills are required due to the rough terrain. This is far and away the most difficult pathfinding exercise in the book.

I think I've made my point. If you like this sort of thing (you know who you are), this is an extraordinary outing, with views so stunning you feel a bit like Sylvester the cat after an unusually bruising encounter with Tweetie-Pie. But you've got to take a positive pleasure in really punishing exercise. Tell a friend where you're going. If you have a mishap, nobody's just going to happen along and find you.

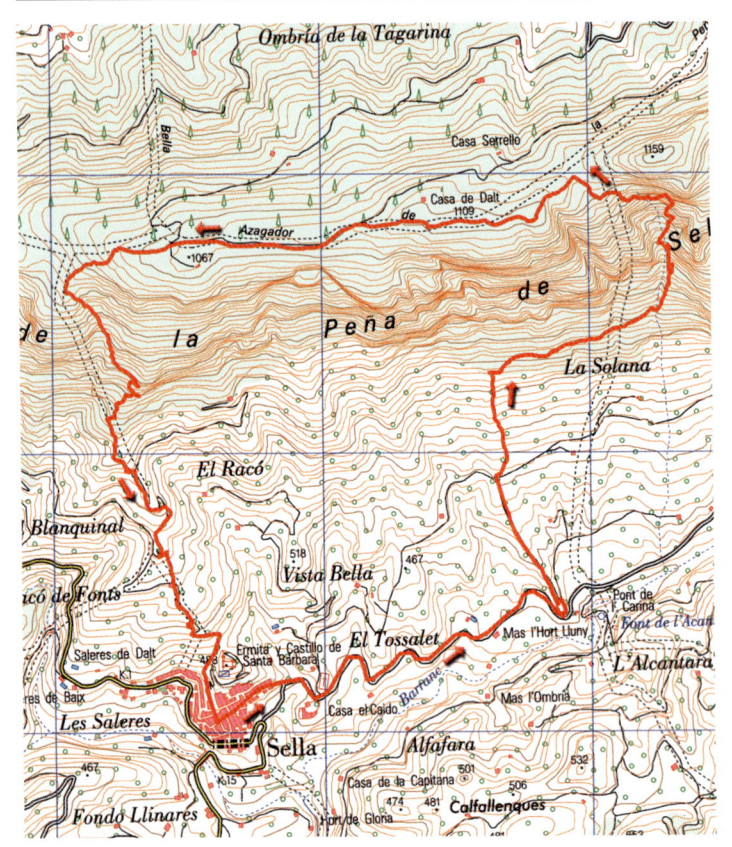

ALTERNATIVE ACCESS AND OTHER WALKS IN THE AREA:

The PR199 includes miles of tarmac and is for the most part eminently drivable. Rather than wearing out your knees, tendons and nerves by walking it, drive up the Tagarina road (on the right as you ascend from Sella toward Puerto de Tudons) to reach several pleasant strolls on dirt tracks, including one (at a sharp left hand bend 6km from the main road) that leads to the Casa del Alt de la Penya de Sella.

GETTING TO THE WALK:

The walk starts from the double car-park below Sella cemetery, 200 metres from the point at which the CV770 arrives in the village from the south. There's a rudimentary mapboard outlining the PRs198 & 199.

THE ROUTE:

Take the Barranc de l'Arc/Font de la Alcantara road round to the right as it passes below the cemetery and in front of the grandiose gateway of a large modern house, and follow it for a little over a kilometre until you come to a 20km speed limit sign at a sharp left hand bend. Leave the road here, climbing to the left on a dirt track identifiable by a *'camino particular'* sign, a waymark on the trunk of a pine tree, and a small sign indicating 'Sella' back along the road (15M).

Follow this track for 50 metres then double back to the left on a rough waymarked branch climbing a long narrow spur, within sight of a house with a sharply raked roof. 50 metres after crossing another asphalted lane at a staggered crossroads (25M), bear right to follow a waymarked route, essentially off path. This is where the pathfinding problems begin and no words can do better than the waymarks, which appear at 30-50 metre intervals. Timings are very subjective since, even if you know where you're meant to be going (I didn't!), you have to cast about for each successive waymark. As a general rule, if you haven't seen a waymark in fifty metres, you've probably strayed off-trail.

After climbing steadily through the scrub and scattered pine in a northerly direction for ten minutes, the way bears right, some 150 metres below the cliffs. A more oblique, north-easterly traverse on a diminishing gradient eventually levels out on a contour (roughly 650 metres) heading east, crossing the first of three watersheds (45M). Continue along the 650-metre contour, crossing a second, slightly deeper watershed (50M), after which sheets of bare rock precede the third, double-channelled watershed (55M).

Once across the third watershed, the way climbs steeply to the left (N), passing between two pine trees, one little, one large, to approach a broad gully at the head of the watershed, the Runar de la Mona (1h15). Progress becomes slightly easier, since the waymarks are more readily visible as we climb very steeply along the right hand side of the scree to an overhang of reddish rock on the right, the Cova de Runar (1h30) - time for a break by anybody's standards!

After the cave, the PR follows the obvious slope to the northwest, climbing through thickening scrub onto a shallow col, within sight of the radar cluttered ridge of the Sierra de Aitana (1h50). Bear left and follow the ridge to the west, still-off path but occasionally passing faint red waymarks, crossing two small rises, the first capped with cairns, the second with a small geodesic survey plaque set in the rock. From here you can see in the distance a clifftop house, the Casa del Alt de la Penya de Sella. Continue west toward the house, descending to join a dirt track 350 metres after the second small rise (2h05).

Follow this track to a crossroads just north of the Casa del Alt de la Penya de Sella (2h15). On guard! A vital bit of pathfinding is imminent, so you've got to have your nose in the book every step of the way, or at least every other step, for the next 750 metres or so. Excuse all the words for ten minutes walking, but you'll understand better on the ground. Detail is your only resource at this point.

Continue straight ahead on a fainter track, passing two pine after 50 metres and the painted number 16 after 100 metres. The track starts to descend toward Collao la Travessa, the col down to your right that, after decades of brushfires, is now submerged in cistus and broom. 200 metres from the crossroads, the track bears left (SW) then swings sharp right, at which point, LEAVE THE TRACK. Don't descend to the col and certainly don't follow the red waymarked path the track feeds into.

Leave the track, passing to the left of a large clump of Holm oak, and descend west, off-path amid scrub and scattered scree, aiming for the arid terraces in the lee of the rocks beyond the col. You'll soon see, on the spur protruding from the near side of the col, two small bushy trees, a pine on the right and a Holm oak on the left. Head for these trees, descending all the while, passing a large cairn with a defaced PR waymark and red boundary markers (a bullseye and the number 25). Sella comes into view as you approach the trees. 50 metres after the trees, bear left, toward Benidorm, still off-path, descending to the head of a wide, steep gully in which, way down to your left, traces of a clear path are discernible (2h25). Congratulations. You've found the way down! The PR descends from this gully to join the dirt track leading to the tall radio mast above Sella, all now clearly visible.

Pick your way down through the scrub, aiming for the clear patch of path on the flank of the gully, and you'll soon find a couple of waymarks. Some care required here, as the descent is very steep and very slippery. Anyone used to walking poles will be glad of them on this stretch. Everyone else proceeds crabwise. After a somewhat precarious descent on an increasingly clear way, cross the scree onto the clear patch of path (2h35). This soon drops down (I use the locution advisedly) onto the splayed, pine fringed spur behind the radio mast. Once on the spur (2h50), a comparatively easy stroll descends more gradually to join the dirt track (3h).

Follow the track down to the radio-mast, ignoring a branch doubling back to the right midway through a chicane. Waymarks disappear again at this stage, but it scarcely matters as the end is in sight and we now simply head for Sella, in particular the Ermita de Santa Barbara, perched on the hill above the village. After a brief stretch on tarmac curving below the mast, double back sharp left on a dirt track. Turn right 30 metres later to descend to 'Vistabella', the recently restored house with a small viewing turret. Keep on descending on a mixture of rough trails and tracks, aiming all the while for the *ermita*, eventually joining a metalled track at the reservoir behind the *ermita*. Descend into Sella and keep descending to the left to return to the starting point.

Costa Blanca Walks   PR.198 Alto de la Penya de Sella - 14

Pas de la Rabosa

15. Cumbre de Aitana

Time:	2h40
Climb:	375 metres
Distance:	10.5km
Grade:	difficult
Access:	by car
Stroll:	Font de la Forata

Miles from the coast, webbed with drivable dirt tracks, and capped with enough satellite dishes to open a soup kitchen for indigent giants, the Cumbre de Aitana may seem a bit of a non-starter for a coastal walking book. However, it is the highest summit in the province, enjoys superb sea views and includes a notorious 'pass' so improbable it has to be seen to be believed, hence its inclusion in the present publication. The difficult grade is for the Pas de la Rabosa, a gateway in the cliff at the top of a rockslide, behind which is a large sinkhole, La Sima de Partagat. In fact, though it looks a little alarming, the route through the rocks is not difficult and is clearly waymarked. Stray off path though and you may find yourself in very precarious straits - first time I did the walk, I missed the waymarks and climbed straight up the rockface, only to find myself stuck in the middle of the sinkhole!

ALTERNATIVE ACCESS

The walk is a variant of the PR20 which, like the PRs 21&22, starts at Puerto dels Tudons on the CV770 between Sella and Alcoleja. However, the first three and a half kilometres are on a perfectly drivable dirt track, and should only be walked if you're suffering an excess of energy or the track is under snow. The walk can also be reached via the PR22 from Confrides on the CV70.

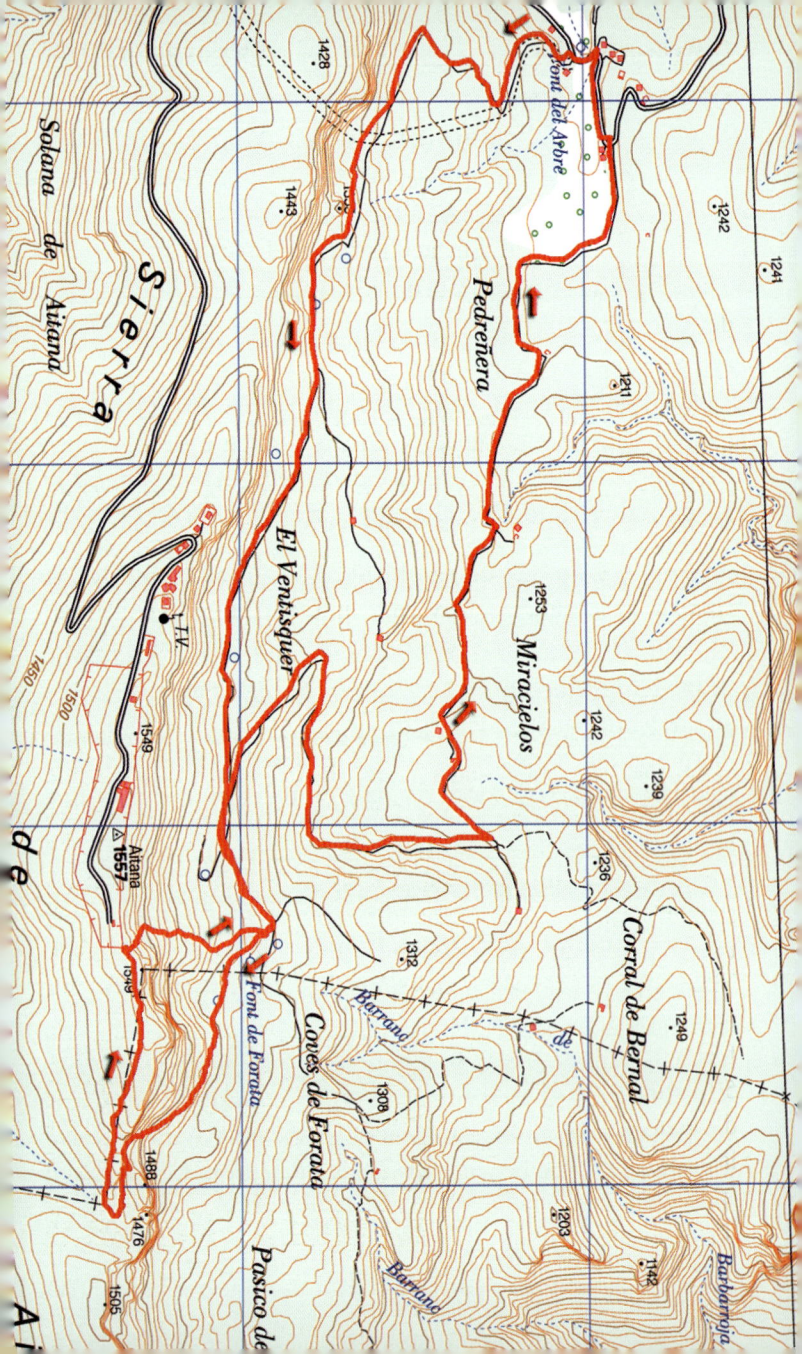

Font del Arbre

1428

1242

1241

1443

Pedreñera

Sierra

1211

Solana de Aitana

El Ventisquer

1253

Miracielos

1549

1242

1239

1236

Aitana
1557

1312

Corral de Bernal

1249

Font de Forata

Costes de Forata

Barranco

1308

de

1488

1203

1142

1476

Pasico de

Barranco

Barbaroja

1505

OTHER WALKS

> PR21   Puerto dels Tudons - Benifato
>
> PR22   Puerto dels Tudons - Confrides (mainly tarmac, all drivable; not to be walked, but a spectacular ride or drive)

The PR21 can be adapted to descend to Benimantell from Font de Partagat

GETTING TO THE WALK

300 metres north of Puerto dels Tudons, take the track (marked with a PR mapboard) climbing to the northeast. Park three-and-a-half kilometres later at the Font de l'Arbre *área recreativa*. If you have to walk it, this stretch takes about 50M.

Alternatively, follow the asphalted PR22 from Confrides. It starts in the middle of the village in front of the 'Caixa Rural' bank. The *área recreativa* is 6.6 kilometres from the village.

THE ROUTE

From the *área recreativa*, take the track climbing to the south, signposted 'Cumbre Aitana 5km'. The track climbs toward the cliffs then veers round to a more easterly direction, passing the first of three *pozos de nieve*, pits in which snow used to be stored for culinary and medicinal use in the Summer (20M). A second snowpit is seen some fifteen minutes later, after which two junctions are passed within fifty metres of one another. The first, which doubles back to the left is the return route. For now, carry straight on then fork left at the Y-junction 50 metres later (40M) to descend to the 'Font de la Forata', named for the 'pierced' rock visible to the southeast (45M).

Pozo de nieve

The PR21 continues along the dirt track. The signpost for the *cumbre* indicates our descent. To tackle the Pas de la Rabosa, take the cairn-marked path (confirmed by a waymark 30 metres later) that climbs from the head of the canalized spring toward the eye in the rock (SE).

The path passes below La Forata, then curves south, petering out at the foot of a small rockslide of large boulders (55M). Follow the waymarks up along the right hand side of the rockslide then bear left, taking care to stick with the waymarked route as it squeezes through the Pas de la Rabosa, two tiny gaps in the rock that act as a gateway into the heart of the mountain (1h05).

Bear left and pick your way over jutting, waymarked stones to a staggered crossroads of paths 100 metres later. Turn right and follow the waymarked route climbing toward the radar station and a summit cairn marking the highest point accessible to the public - the trig point is inside the military installations. The descent, unmarked for the first 100 metres, starts at the northeastern corner of the military compound (1h25).

A rough but obvious way zigzags down to the hanger of pine at the foot of the escarpment. Turn right at the pine and follow the narrow path descending steeply along the edge of the wood (some care required if the path is rimed with frost) back to Font de la Forata (1h40).

From the spring, you can either return via the same track or, for a more circuitous but more picturesque route, fork right at the second (in this direction of walking) of the two junctions west of the spring. Simply follow this track as it winds its way down into the valley, ignoring a branch off to the right at a sharp bend (2h05). The track eventually joins the Confrides road a couple of hundred metres from the Font de l'Arbre.

Costa Blanca Walks — Cumbre de Aitana - 15

16 - PR.15 Barranco del Salt — Costa Blanca Walks

View Northwest

16. PR15 Barranco del Salt

Time:	4h45
Climb:	850 metres
Distance:	17km
Grade:	medium to difficult
Access:	by car or (adding 5km rtn.) on foot from Polop
Short Version:	starting from La Casa de Dios if your tyres and clutch are ready to take the requisite punishment.

PR making at its finest, this great circuit gives every impression of being an agreeable stroll along drivable dirt tracks then, just when you're thinking, "Well, it's all very nice, but...", it catches you unawares with a hugely improbable path climbing below looming cliffs to a delightful mountain enclave. More striking still is the tranquillity. Given the abrupt nature of the Costa Blanca mountains and the ubiquity of the boys from the blackstuff, many comparatively wild places are polluted by a background hum of traffic, but on this itinerary there are moments where the silence is absolute. Even the air traffic controllers seem to have selected flight paths in deference to the mountain. Benidorm round the corner? Don't be daft, it's on a different planet!

The walking is easy throughout and the itinerary only merits a medium-difficult grade for length and the intimidating grandeur of the landscape. Distance is slightly flexible as it is possible (in a comparatively light car with plenty of torque) to drive to La Casa de Dios. The PR officially begins in Polop. Our proposed starting point is a compromise between indolence and an urge to preserve the clutch.

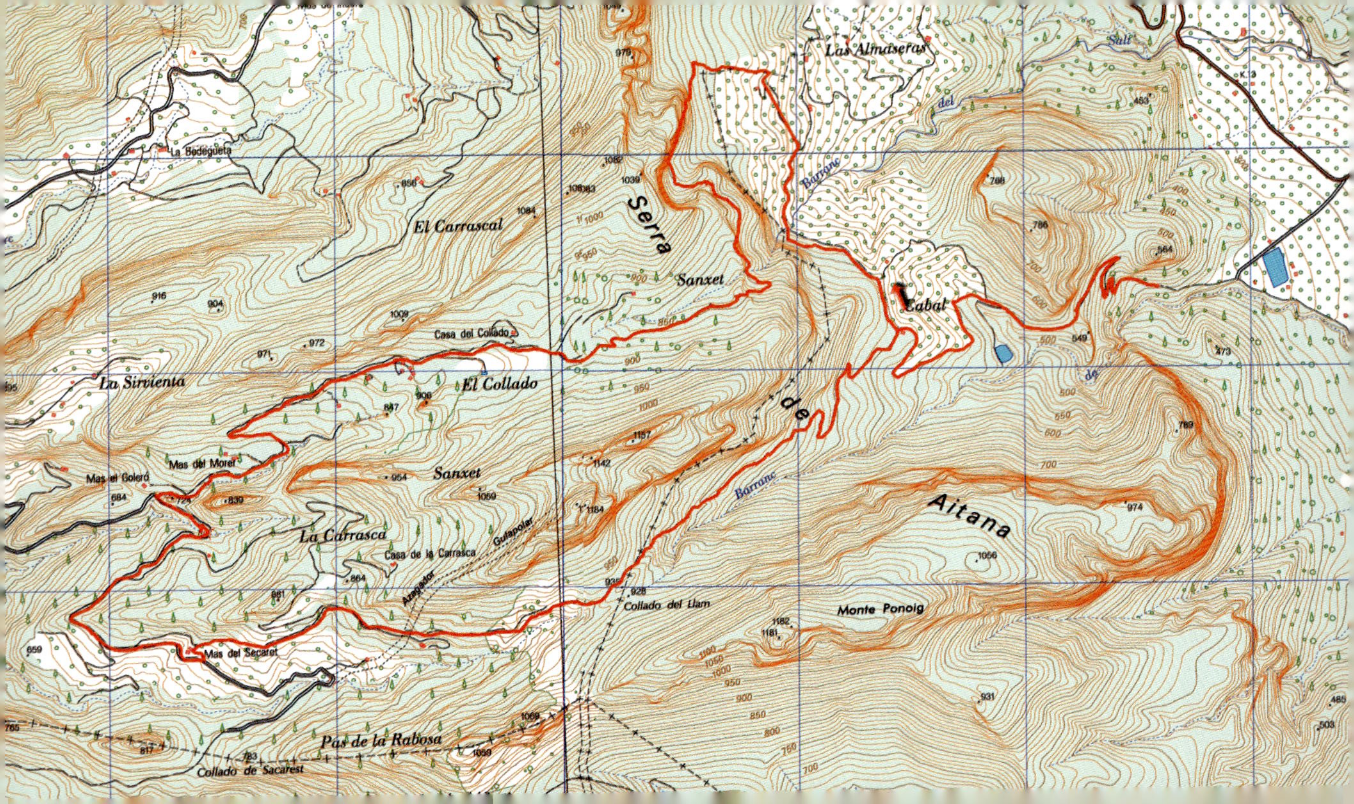

La Bodegueta
El Carrascal
Serra de Aitana
Sanxet
Las Almaseras
Barranc del Sull
Barranc de Cabal
Casa del Collado
El Collado
La Sirvienta
Mas del Morer
Mas el Goleró
La Carrasca
Casa de la Carrasca
Gulapolar
Azagador
Collado del Llam
Monte Ponoig
Mas del Secaret
Pas de la Rabosa
Collado de Sacarest

ALTERNATIVE ACCESS

For alternative access, see Walk 13. The 2h50 point can be reached in a normal car without too much grief for tyres and clutch by continuing on the dirt track after the climbers' refuge until you come to the signposted turning for Polop via Salt.

OTHER WALKS
    PR13   to Finestrat

GETTING TO THE WALK

The official start for the PRs 13, 15, 16 & 17 is the 'Camí de Bovalar', which is 500 metres along the CV715 between Polop and Benimantell/Guadalest, just after the 'Chirles' turning.

Take the asphalted lane, setting the odometer at 0 and follow the PR waymarks, crossing the CV70 after 900 metres. Continue on the lane that initially runs parallel to the main road before curving round the Bovalar orange grove into the Barranco de Gulapdar. Continue on the track when the tarmac ends at km1.9, fork left at km2.1 and park in the cutting beside the track at km2.5.

THE ROUTE

Continue on the same track on foot, climbing steadily to a cutting below cliffs favoured by local climbers, and another possible parking place (15M). From here, the fine manifold summit of Sanxet comes into view, and you can see the grey-blue walls of La Casa de Dios, where the loop begins. Ignore all branch tracks and follow the main, well stabilized track as it climbs past a reservoir.

At La Casa de Dios (40M), the main signposted route lies to the left. This is our return route. For the present, continue on the main track, following a contour before dipping down toward terraced slopes and a major junction (1h). Take the chained fork climbing on the left toward a small house, just below which, our itinerary bears right on a narrow cairn and waymarked path traversing a terrace (1h05).

The path veers left at the end of the terrace and climbs steadily, passing a ruin before reaching a T-junction, at which point we turn left (1h15). This is where it all gets a little improbable. As far as one can see, there's nothing but a lot of dirty great cliffs lying ahead, but in fact a clear and easy path (though none the less spectacular for its clarity and facility) passes below the outermost pinnacle visible to the south.

The path follows the line of a partially interred black pipe, climbing steadily below towering cliffs, then levels out briefly before climbing again, traversing an escarpment that looks like it's only just popped out of the ground. After a rocky pass below the pinnacle (1h35), a dizzying but well-made path snakes along under a menacing overhang and the scar of a dry waterfall (the eponymous 'Salt'), now siphoned off at source. Beyond the falls, a series of traverses (looking distinctly precipitous from afar, but beautifully judged once you're on them) zigzag up to a pass into a terraced enclave cradling the derelict Sanxet farm (2h).

A gentle stroll (W) traversing abandoned almond terraces takes us past the ruin and onto a narrow track that climbs to join a broader track beside a helipad, just short of a large shuttered house, Mas El Collado (2h15). Take the track to the west, passing behind the house, where the present itinerary intersects with Walk 13. Follow the main track, ignoring all branches, as it descends past cabins and cottages to the Finestrat-Sella track (2h50).

Turn left and head toward Finestrat, climbing briefly then following a contour amid densely planted pine, at the end of

a menacing overhang...

which there's a metal barrier against traffic, where fine views open out over Els Castellets and Puig Campana (3h05). Ignore minor forks to right and left and stay on the main track, passing below a long bungalow, the Caserio de Zacarets, immediately after which, at a clearly signposted junction, the PR turns sharp left (3h15) to climb directly behind the bungalow.

A rough track that erosion and scrub are set upon reducing to a trail climbs intermittently, passing behind a ruin before dwindling to a waymarked path (3h35) leading to the Collado de Llam and the junction of the PRs 15, 16 & 17 (3h45). From here, all that remains is a good old gallop down the mountain, initially on a narrow, clearly waymarked path, then (4h) on the minor track back to La Casa de Dios (4h15).

17 - Monte Ponoig from Finestrat Costa Blanca Walks

Summit cross and Benidorm

17. Monte Ponoig from Finestrat

Time:	4h30
Climb:	850 metres
Distance:	14km (rtn.)
Grade:	medium
Access:	by car or on foot from Finestrat
Stroll:	Refugio de Tio Frare

Ponoig, commonly dubbed El Leon Dormido or The Sleeping Lion, is one of the Costa Blanca classics, only marginally less celebrated than its mighty neighbour, Puig Campana. It's normally approached via the Barranco de Gulapdar or Taberna de Margoch, respectively the PRs 16 & 17.

The first route is amply covered in Walk 16 and we had intended tackling the summit via Margoch, but at the time of writing the early stages of this approach are being submerged in a faintly insane *urbanizacion* project (get stuck inside it and you feel you'll never get out again) rendering the 'getting to the walk' section indescribable. Hence this roundabout approach via the PR289, the traditional tour of Puig Campana.

Unfortunately, since the fire in March 2006, the full circuit involves a long stretch of burnt forest, hence as with Puig Campana, you should drive up the road first to see how far the western flank of the mountain has recovered before embarking on the complete tour. If it looks grim, treat this as a linear two-way return or adapt it (see text) as a one-way traverse of the sierras dividing Finestrat and Polop, both of which can be reached by bus from Benidorm. Whatever you do, though, don't just strike it off your list. This is a great walk and heartily recommended. The itinerary is well waymarked and clearly signposted and, for the most part, follows good

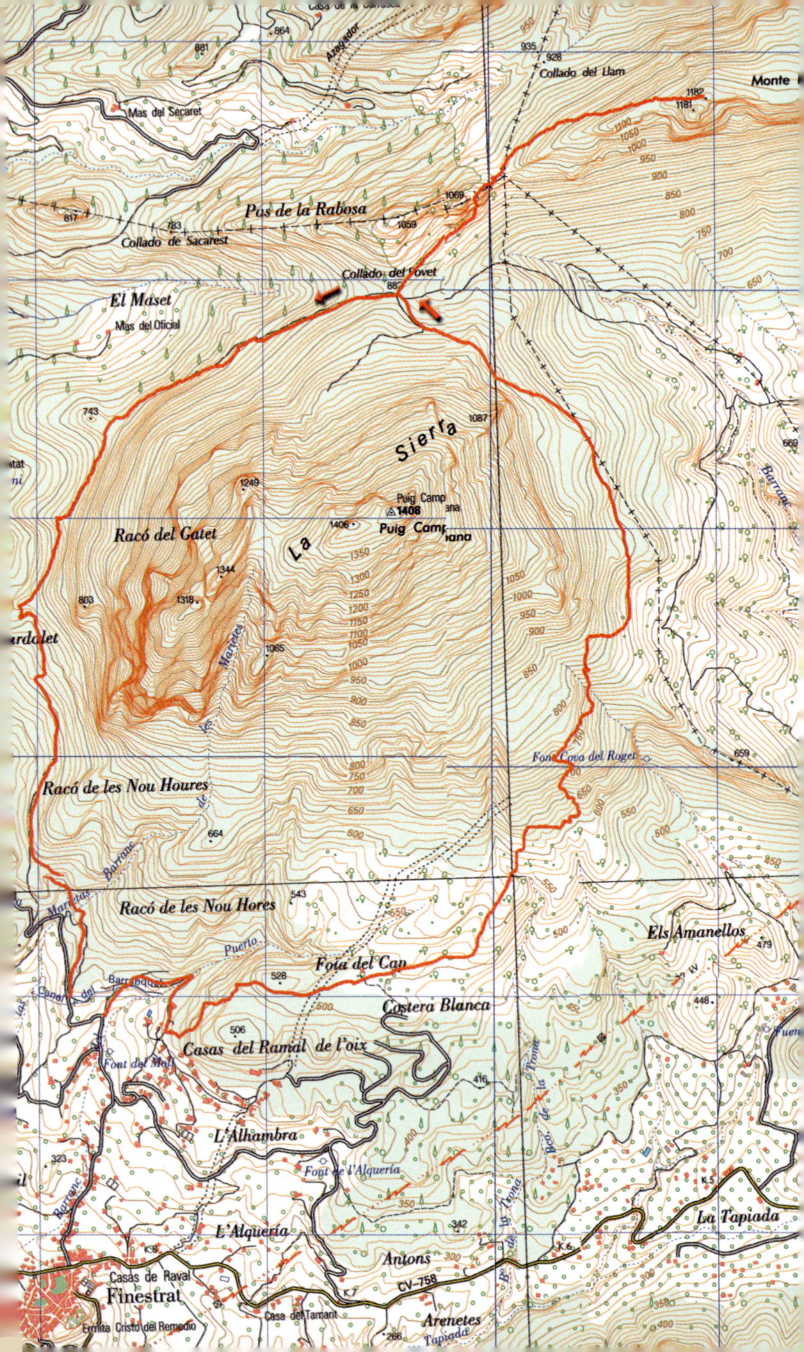
Monte
Collado del Llam
Mas del Secaret
Azagador
Pas de la Rabosa
Collado de Sacarest
Collado del Povet
El Maset
Mas del Oficial
La Sierra
Puig Campana
Racó del Gatet
Manetes
Font Cova del Roget
Racó de les Nou Houres
Barranc de Manetes
Racó de les Nou Hores
Puerto
Foia del Can
Els Amanellos
Costera Blanca
Casas del Ramal de l'oix
Font del Mal
L'Alhambra
Font de l'Alquería
L'Alquería
La Tapiada
Antons
CV-758
Casas de Raval
Finestrat
Casa del Tamant
Arenetes
Ermita Cristo del Remedio
Tapiada

paths. Description is correspondingly brief and chiefly serves as a means of pacing progress.

ALTERNATIVE ACCESS:

From Polop, see Walk 16 plus the PRs 16 & 17

OTHER WALKS IN THE AREA:

See Walk 12

GETTING TO THE WALK:

From the centre of Finestrat, follow the brown signs for 'Font del Molí' and park in the *área recreativa* car-park just after the *fuente*.

THE ROUTE

From the first bend above the *area recreativa*, take the broad, badly eroded track climbing to the northeast. Turn right after the canal 200 metres later and follow the main track as it climbs past a couple of villas then, just before the track joins an asphalted road, fork left on a broad, clearly waymarked path (15M).

The path climbs steadily through the woods for ten minutes before levelling off and crossing a turning circle at the end of a dirt track (30M). After recrossing the track 275-metres later (the Refugio Pedre de Tio Frare is signposted to the left), the PR continues on a pleasant terrace path, passing a ruin with a troglodytic annex. From the end of the terrace, a long, gentle climb takes us past a red waymarked path climbing from the right (50M).

Shortly after the junction, our path emerges from the woods and climbs steadily across a rocky, scrub clad hillside. After a little over twenty minutes, you'll come to the rise of a broad spur, from where the Bernia ridge and, off to your left, Monte Ponoig come into view. The PR skirts a large sinkhole at the top of the spur (1h25), then slowly curves round to the northwest, climbing intermittently but generally following contours before joining the track descending from Puig Campana, 200 metres above the confluence of paths on Coll de Pouet.

Descend to the coll (2h) and turn right on the path climbing to the northeast, forking right at the Y-junction after 375 metres to cross an old overgrown rockslide. At the signposted junction on the ridge overlooking Collado del Llam (2h15), turn right and follow the clearly waymarked route climbing steadily, mostly on good paths amid attractive clumps of Holm oak, along the northern escarpment to the cross on the summit of Monte Ponoig (2h45).

After enjoying the views, retrace your steps to the last signposted junction (3h05), taking care on the loose stones. You now have a choice of itineraries. If the fire-damage on the western flank of Puig Campana has begun to repair itself, return to Coll de Pouet and follow Walk 12 option A back to Font del Molì. If the fire damage remains bad and you're obliged to return to Finestrat, go back the same way (there is an alternative via Collado del Llam and the PR12 between Sella and Finestrat, but this involves an unconscionable amount of time on tarmac). If you want to do a linear traverse to Polop, turn right and follow the PR waymarked path down to Collado de Llam (ignoring two forks on the left) and the signposted junction with the Casa de Dios path (3h15) (see Walk 16 for details).

Costa Blanca Walks — Monte Ponoig from Finestrat - 17

View over Gulapdar

18 - Sierra de Aixorta **Costa Blanca Walks**

View of Bernia

18. Sierra de Aixorta

Time:	5h15
Climb:	750 metres
Distance:	20km
Grade:	difficult
Access:	by car, though it could be adapted to start from Callosa or Bolulla by using the PR49, which is outlined in a leaflet available at Callosa Tourist Information Office
Stroll:	drive to the end of the tarmac and follow the track to the orchard behind Paso Tancat.

The Sierra de Aixorta is a splendid little range of mountains separating the Guadalest valley from the enclave of Castell de Castells. Despite some fine sea views, it isn't exactly coastal, but I wanted to include at least one itinerary in the area to give you an idea of the hinterland's potential, hence this roundabout route designed to provide a glimpse of as many options as possible. Five PRs are crossed or used, but rather more interesting are the countless unofficial routes that crisscross the range, one of which is used in our descent.

The latter are often rough and only sketchily waymarked with fading dots or the odd cairn, but they're nearly always worth exploring if you're prepared to spend a little time puzzling out where the path is. That proviso is significant. Many of these paths are obscure and the present itinerary is only recommended for confident pathfinders who are happy committing themselves to a way that looks like it's going nowhere fast. Length and obscurity are the reasons for the difficult grade. If walking alone, tell someone where you're going.

La Solana
Pla de Dalt
Coll de Bixauca
Pouet de les Peres
CV-752
Corral del Visentico
El Somo
Penya Escoda
Corral del Somo
Alt del Somo
Corral del Pi Bertol
Corral de Salvoret Bataller
El Coscollar
Corral de Poll
Pla del Xarquet
Corrales de Garach
Aljub del Xarquet
Corral del Xarquet
La Foia del Clot
Garx
El Pouet
Muntanya
Corral de Revuelto
Casa de Bixauca
Bixauca
Casa de Salvà
El Pou
Font d'Olbis
Buscarró
Albicà
Font d'Albicà
Benipla
Serral
Font de Benisa
La Clapissa
Costera del Pubil
Serra del Racó Roig
Espinar
Racó del Xarquet
Font de la Teja
Lloma del Sacanyar
Costera del Racó
Sacanyar
Font del Garx
Pas Tancat
Sarroxa
Penya del Castellet
Tossalet de Miquelet Monjó
Penya de Tàrbena
Tàrbena
Poble Dalt (Ruinas)
El Collado
Costera del Caro
Barranc Negre
Cerro de los Parats
Font Major
Foia de la Font Major
d'Aixorta
Morro Blau
Xorta
Foia de Salvà
Sarrotxa
Vinyes
El Pinar
Foia Sellés
Foia Pla
Els Blanquinals
CV-715
El Matapoll
Pla de Codolla
Rastrel de la Solana
Penya l'Or

OTHER WALKS IN THE AREA
From Callosa d'en Sarrià:
*ET PR44	Benifato & Confrides
PR45	Pantano de Guadalest & Confrides
*PR46	Tàrbena & Castell de Castells
*ET PR47	La Nucia
*PR49	Senda Vella to Castell de Castells

From Tarbena:
PR145	Serrals & Parelles via Font dels Olbis
PR146	Cami de ses Roques & Pica-sàries

From Guadalest:
*ET PR18	Cumbre de Xortà
ET PR19	Castell de Castells

From Castell de Castells:
PR149	Penya del Castellet
*PR150	Morro Blau
*PR151	Els Arcs
PR168	Barranco de Malafi

* Itineraries marked with an asterisk are partially used in the present walk.

ET stands for 'Excessive tarmac'. These itineraries spend far too much time on the road and are only recommended if you're desperate for an outing on a really wild winter's day. Even then I make no claims for the pleasure quotient.

GETTING TO THE WALK

Take the unnumbered road climbing to the NW from between kms46&47 (36&37 on the Military Map) of the CV715, 700 metres north of Bolulla, setting the odometer at 0 as you leave the main road. The walk starts at the junction with the concrete track at km2.1. There's a clear parking bay on the right 100 metres later, otherwise park alongside the road. Roadside parking is tight, but so long as you're sensible about it, shouldn't be a problem.

THE ROUTE

Follow the road as it climbs steeply for 600 metres then, just after the first sharp left hand bend, turn right on a mule trail marked with cairns. The trail crosses terraces, then dwindles to a path winding between pine before rejoining the road where the tarmac gives way to dirt track (20M). Continue on the dirt track as it climbs between a ruin and a recently built house, then bears right, descending into the valley behind the dramatic declivity of Paso Tancat (literally 'closed pass'). Ignore a turning on the right at the end of a stretch of concrete (35M) and fork left, then left again 50 metres later, heading north on a rough track that descends to a delightful orchard framed by dramatic valleys and gorges (45M).

Castell de Castells

Continue on the track as it climbs out of this privileged spot, leading to the end of a tarmac lane (1h05) within sight of the Tarbená/Castell de Castells road, the CV752. Follow this lane for 500 metres until it swings sharp right (1h10), then double back to the left on a rough trail leading to a PR-waymarked (PR46) track, which at this stage is surfaced with concrete. Follow this track to the west, traversing terraces of olive and almond trees, ignoring all branches. Track and road run in tandem, only briefly diverging at a narrow gully, until the track joins the road just short of Collado de Bichauca (1h40). Turn left and follow the road for 1.4 kilometres - too much, I know, but not a lot by local PR standards!

Just short of the km7 milestone, turn left on a broad dirt track, signposted 'Fonts del Teixos 9km'/ 'PR151 Els Arcs 2.6km' (2h05). With the exception of one shortcut, we follow this track all the way to the Fonts del Teixos *área recreativa*, enjoying fine views and taking note of the alternative walks passed en route. Midway across a terraced basin, a PR151 diversion forks left for 'Aljib Xorquet', an *aljib* or *aljub* being a reservoir of Arabic origin (2h25). Beyond the basin, the PR151 forks right for 'Penya Escoda' (2h35). We stay on the main track as it climbs into the Sierra de Aixorta, traversing three short stretches of concrete.

At the end of the third stretch of concrete, 4.5 kilometres from Fonts del Teixos via the main track, turn left on a steep, stony branch track climbing to the south (3h). This track levels out in a terraced bowl, on the far side of which it veers right and resumes climbing, and two minor branches fork off to the left (3h10). Turn left on the higher of the two branch tracks and follow it until it ends at an abandoned spring. Maintain direction on a narrow path that dips into an eroded watershed below the scar of the main Fonts del Teixos track, which is now running along the base of the Cumbre de Aixorta's northern cliffs. Ignore the eroded way descending to the left and maintain an easterly direction on the higher traces of several infinitely faint goat tracks (if in doubt just climb directly off path) to recover the main track 75-metres later (3h20), joining the PRs 18&150.

Follow the track up to a junction just below the *área recreativa* and fork left, staying on the PR150 (3h40). Fork left again 500 metres later (3h45) then, 300 metres after that, turn left at the wreck of an old car sporting a 'Brittany Ferries GB' sticker, ignoring the PR cross (3h49). This rough branch track looks like it's going to peter out above a sheer drop, but 45 metres after a couple of tin baths on your left, you'll see on your right a yellow waymark and cairns framing the start of a tiny, very faint path, which is where your pathfinding skills are required (3h55).

Taking care to follow the clearer patches of path and looking out for cairns and yellow waymarks, descend steadily (E) amid young pine and spiny broom, heading all the while for the sharp summit on the Bernia ridge. Cairns indicate the way over a slew of rocks (4h05), after which a slightly clearer path descends steeply across ancient terracing, passing a couple of old PR waymarks, though this is not an official PR. The path then runs onto the southern flank of the valley (4h15), from where the 20M point is visible off to the left.

The path remains narrow, but becomes much clearer as it descends toward the patchwork of nets covering the medlar orchards around Callosa. It eventually joins a rough dirt track near a small byre/corral (4h35) where life becomes considerably easier. Turn left and simply follow this track all the way back to the start of the walk, passing en route a small open cabin (4h55) and two cairn-marked tracks doubling back to the right.

Costa Blanca Walks — Sierra de Aixorta - 18

The way down seen from below

Sunset over the Sierra de Bernia

19. Sierra de Bèrnia

Time:	2h40
Climb:	310 metres
Distance:	7.7km
Grade:	medium
Access:	by car
Short Version:	to the fort, returning by the same route

The Sierra de Bèrnia enjoys an exalted reputation among Costa Blanca ramblers. Personally, I'm not persuaded it's all it's cracked up to be, but only in Spain, Europe's second most mountainous country, could one become so blasé as to be a bit sniffy about such a fine mountain!

And on this, the classic loop of the PR7, we encounter at least one genuinely miraculous phenomenon, the famous 'forat', a fifteen metre natural tunnel through the mountain. These 'perforations' are quite common in northeastern Spain, but few are as neatly formed as this narrow subway, which is so low that you have to get down on hands and knees -wet knees most likely- if you want to go through it.

The walk is relatively easy, but gets a medium grade for the rough ground on the southern flank and for the crawling. There's little risk of vertigo, but a slight danger of claustrophobia in the tunnel.

The mapboard suggests doing the walk in the opposite direction, but this way round, the tunnel comes as a fitting climax to the itinerary, and for those who don't want to dirty their knees, the fort is an attractive objective for a short walk.

Pas dels Bandolers
Pas del Racó Ample
Morro Penyal
Racó de la Segaissa
Morro de l'Aspre
Caserio de Bernia
Casa del Bancal Llarga
Bancal Llarga
Casa de la Concepción
Casas de Berdiola
Lloma Ll
Curt
del
Bernia
1126
1104
999
1007
986
888
989
985
947
976
912
812
819
744
784
627
618
641
626
545
542
491
482
609
643
K.12
K.13
El Fort
Font del Fort
L. L. Provisional
Risco del Portezuelo
de
Bérnia
Ermita del Vicario
Gato
1000
950
900
800
700
650
600
550
500
460

Costa Blanca Walks   Sierra de Bèrnia - 19

ALTERNATIVE ACCESS & OTHER WALKS:

The PR7 loop can also be joined via its official start in Altea La Vella or via the PR48 from Callosa d'en Sarrià. If taking the latter option, drive past the Fonts d'Algar and start at the track forking off the road above the *Museu d'Agua/zona de acampada*. A longer loop mostly on dirt track can be done round the eastern end of the sierra. It's also possible to climb the main western summit and Penya Severino from the pass above the fort.

GETTING TO THE WALK:

Access is via the CV749, either from the CEPSA/ELF station at Jalón/Xaló or climbing via 'Pinos' shortly after the Xaló road leaves the N332. Park after the junction of the two branches of the CV749 at the 'Serra Bèrnia' bar/restaurant, where the dark tarmac gives way to paler asphalt.

THE ROUTE

From the restaurant, continue along the asphalted track for a little over 100 metres, then fork right at the mapboard to maintain a southwesterly direction on a dirt track, traversing terraces of vine, almond and olive. The track climbs to the pine fringed foot of the ridge, bringing Tàrbena into view, after which it traverses fire-ravaged slopes carpeted with cistus. As you approach the long shoulder above Paso de los Bandoleros, cairns mark an easy shortcut (25M) that rejoins the track shortly before it dwindles to a path (30M).

Follow the path south, toward Penya Severino, until it climbs gently to a rocky col accessing the southern side of the mountain (50M), where another waymarked route climbs to the left toward the western summit. Continue along the main path (SE) and, 175 metres later, you'll find the ruins of the sixteenth century Fort de Bèrnia, which enjoys fine views of Puig Campana,

Monte Ponoig, and the Sierra Helada. It's worth spending a few minutes here (not counted in subsequent timings) moochingabout and reading the multilingual information panels. One of the eastern vaults is still intact and clean enough to function as a refuge.

Head east on the main waymarked path, bringing into view the more dramatic seaward pinnacles silhouetted against the Mediterranean. Rough ground ensues and some care is required on the sharper limestone clints as you pick your way across the rock toward the end of a minor road. After a metre-high drop (bottom and hands maybe required), the waymarked route crosses two tongues of fallen rock, climbing along the nearside of the second slide, where the PR7 from Altea La Vella feeds into the main loop from the right (1h10).

After a third rockslide, a clearer, well-trodden path climbs to the east, bringing the western pinnacles of El Portet, which had briefly disappeared, back into view. Another stretch of rough limestone and some more bottoms-down stuff precede a large solitary oak set in a sweep of debris (1h25). Continue on the PR, descending very slightly before a good dirt path climbs back toward El Portet, going through a 'gateway' in front of a cave composed of crumbling agglomerate (1h40).

Waymarks indicate the way across massive boulders (you wouldn't want to have been here when they broke away from the cliff) onto a clear path climbing to the undisputed marvel of this itinerary, the natural tunnel of the *forat* (2h). Dogs proceed normally, the rest of us crawl. Once through the tunnel, a good dirt path runs along the northern flank of the ridge, almost immediately passing a large, attractive cave. Thereafter, a straightforward descent leads to the Fuente de Bèrnia and the dirt track, which we follow back to the start.

fellow ramblers...

20 - Les Mamelles de la Solana

Looking inland from the top

20. The Breasts On The Sunny Side Of The Mountain

Time:	3h25
Climb:	400 metres
Distance:	14km
Grade:	medium
Access:	by car or (see alternative access) on foot from Benissa
Short Version:	Sella de Cau. To reach the 1h10 point by car, take the tarmac lane forking off the CV749 (Pinos branch) at km18.4, 8.7km from the junction with the CV750 (Benissa to Xalo).

No, I'm not making the name up to satisfy a smutty sense of humour. Nor is it the title of a seventies self-help manual mixing cod mysticism with the dogmas of sexual liberation. Simply a straightforward translation of the traditional tag for the twin peaks of the Sierra de la Solana, 'Les Mamelles de la Solana'. Often ignored by ramblers rushing to get to the top of more dramatic ridges, this is a delightfully domestic landscape, dotted with well-maintained terraces and attractive houses, and boasting at least one view that is the equal to any on the Costa Blanca. Domesticity does have its drawbacks though, in this instance 2.5km on tarmac, but once you've seen the views, I don't imagine you'll take exception to the asphalt.

ALTERNATIVE ACCESS:

The Ayuntamiento de Benissa (www.benissa.net) publish a pamphlet in mildly surreal English detailing the 'PR Solana', a linear variant of the present itinerary climbing from Benissa via the Rafalet farmhouse, which is at km25.3 of the CV749 (Pinos branch).

Planeta de la Casa de Maseraf
Casa del Siores
Repelat
Coves de Carraxet
Maseraf
Corral de Carachel
Barranquet
Les Planisses
Morro de la Ventolana
Casa de Planises
Casa del Repelat
Casa de la Ventola
Tossal Roig
Sierra de la Venta
Plana del Single
Alt de les Planisses
Penyes Rojes
Casa Escalès
Lloma Plana
Les Plantses
Ermita de Marne (ruinas)
Casa Vicenta
Cases de Calite
Sella del Ca
Tossal del Navarro
El Fondo
La Solana
CV-749
El Conquet
Caserío de Marnes
Marnés
Marnes
Casa de Marnes
Tossal de l'Aspre
Barranc del Aspre
Lloma la Cova
Casa del Conquet
Corral del Co
Mamellers de Lleus
Tossal de Pinos
Pinos

GETTING TO THE WALK:

The walk starts shortly before the junction of the two branches of the CV749 and can be begun from the *Zona de Acampada* (a rough dirt track climbing to the left after the km12 milepost as you approach from Xalo), or from either of the two restaurants in the next few hundred metres, the 'Bon Vent' and 'Vista Bernia'.

THE ROUTE:

At the southern end of the camping area, where the track curves west toward the road, a faint path heads southwest, passing behind the 'Bon Vent' restaurant before descending to the 'Refugio Vista Bernia' (5M). Bear left, passing in front of the restaurant, and follow a rough dirt track descending past two cabins - a lot of barking and tail-wagging here. When the track ends at the second cabin, continue descending on a rough path onto a broad spur overlooking a dirt track. Fork left when the path divides midway along the spur (10M), maintaining a north-easterly direction on the rougher but less overgrown branch.

This path apparently peters out 100 metres later at the head of abandoned terraces, 50 metres short of a ruin with a powder blue wall. Some care required here. The way down to the track doesn't appear on maps. Looking at the lay of the land, I guessed it must exist, located it on the eve of doing the walk, but had trouble finding it again the next day! Turn left on the top terrace and you'll find a rough way winding down the terraces to a strip field behind the powder blue ruin. This field may be ploughed, but it's only a few metres short of the dirt track seen from above.

Once on the track (15M), turn left and follow it as it contours round the mountain below the Penyes Rojes cliffs, passing Casa Escales and crossing the Loma Plana spur before descending

Les Mamelles

into the Marnes valley. After nearly half an hour on the track, the working farmhouses and immaculately maintained terraces give way to renovated, expat residences and the track joins a tarmac lane (50M).

Turn left and follow this lane for a little over a kilometre until it switches back through a chicane, and the trig point on Sella de Cau comes into view as you pass a large house fronted with a large and largely superfluous (it doesn't actually enclose anything at its southern end) wall. This is a useful landmark for both short and long versions of the itinerary. If in doubt (the wall may well be extended one day), the smaller house opposite is called 'Casa Cipres' and is identified as such by a ceramic plaque on its northern face.

50 metres after these two houses, turn right on a track (1h10) climbing toward a yellow-painted house with a satellite dish on the hillside behind it. This track climbs all the way to the col between the Mamelles, but the two large bends looping round the yellow house can be cut. For the first shortcut, turn left 200 metres from the lane on a branch track leading to a ruin, then cut across a terrace to rejoin the main track. When the track doubles back to the yellow house, maintain direction on a rough path climbing steeply to the northeast. 125-metres later, a line of stones on the right steers you back onto the track (1h20). Follow the track to a Y-junction and fork left, skirting the base of the more southerly 'breast', Tossal del Navarro, until the track ends at a cabin and breeze-block byre below the larger 'breast', Sella de Cau (1h35). Behind the byre a rough but clear and clearly waymarked path climbs steeply to the Sella de Cau trig-point, from where we enjoy a splendid 360° panorama, superior to that from many a higher mountain (1h50).

Retrace your steps to the byre (2h) and a choice of routes back to the large walled house, the choice depending on the stronger impulse in your own particular walking make-up: fiend for a loop or an asphalt-phobe? I'm afraid you have to opt for one or the other! If the asphalt-phobia is stronger, follow the same track back to the walled house. For the loop, which involves an extra kilometre on tarmac, take the narrow waymarked path to the right behind the byre, descending to a track that rejoins the lane a couple of hundred metres later. Turn left to return to the walled house (2h30).

At the southern end of the wall, just above the chicane, fork right, leaving the lane and taking a *very* narrow path (the official pamphlet describes this as "a path for cavalry") weaving between exposed rock. The path is confirmed by a small cairn after a few metres and, more permanently, 100 metres from the road, a gap in a low wall with a red boundary waymark including the number 3.

Once you're on this path, it's relatively easy to follow as it winds across a plateau spattered with orchids and blowsy looking iris (SW) toward the tree fringed rise of the *zona de acampada*. Bear left at an inverted Y-junction (2h40), descending back toward Marnes for 250 metres to the low walls of a ruin, beyond which the path resumes its southwesterly direction along a narrow, rocky terrace. Fork right at the faint Y-junction after the terrace (2h45) to stay on the clearer traces, still descending slightly, within sight of the houses passed before first joining the lane. As the path approaches the terraces behind the higher of these houses, fork right at a clearly waymarked Y-junction (2h50) and climb toward the stand of pine on the horizon. Now that it's perfectly obvious, the path is well waymarked with yellow and occasionally red dots, as it meanders through the scrub, climbing gently and eventually passing to the left of the stand of pine, beyond which it briefly joins a rough dirt track (3h10).

The track almost immediately bears left to end at a roofless ruin, while we maintain a westerly direction, following old paths descending toward an abandoned house and sentry-box well. Pass directly in front of the house and continue southwest for the final brief climb into the *zona de acampada*.

Costa Blanca Walks — Les Mamelles de la Solana - 20

View back toward Bernia

Font d'Aixa

21. Castell de Aixa

Time:	3h20
Climb:	450 metres
Distance:	8.25km
Grade:	medium-difficult
Access:	by car

If you read the introduction, you may recall that I spent a bit of time banging on about how generous the Spanish are with their pathmaking. No group though could be more bighearted than the Centro Excursionista Pedreguer. Faced with the task of mapping a PR (note the singular article) and given one relatively modest mountain in which to do it, the Sierra de Castell de la Solana, they went haring off all over the place with their pots of paint, waymarking every last patch of path they could lay their hands on, and came up with no less than five itineraries for the one number. Such liberality can be a little confusing on the ground, but you've got to admire them for entering into the spirit of the thing.

The present itinerary, with its rather out of the way start and frequent intersections, is designed to give the best introduction to this network of paths, touching on all of them (except the PR53.4) at least briefly. The walk was researched in drizzle and dense mist, which wasn't ideal, but too much sun wouldn't be desirable either as, despite being dotted with wells, this is a dry mountain that has suffered countless fires over the years. The paths are well waymarked, but often badly overgrown with thorny scrub (come up here with a Strimmer and you could make yourself very popular indeed), for which reason long trousers and long sleeves are essential for anyone not of a strongly masochistic bent.

osa
EL Molló
CV-720
K.6
Barranc
El Romput
Castellet de L'Ocaive
Ocaive
404
Puets
383
376
493
347
Muntanya Grand
503
506
Font d'Aixa
291
257
Tossal de la Llosa
524
513
iquasi
uasi
Castell D'Aixa
607
Barranc
de
la
La Fontadacha

ALTERNATIVE ACCESS:

The main path can also be joined either from Carrer Cid or Parc del Patronat in Pedreguer, and Fonts del Ombreta and Tia Xima on the CV733 between Pedreguer and Alcanali.

OTHER WALKS IN THE AREA:

For further explorations, a general map and detailed leaflets describing individual paths (in Catalan) are available from the Ayuntament de Pedreguer and the Vall de Pop tourist information office in Xalo.

>   PR53.   Sendero de Pedreguer
>   PR53.   1 Pedreguer to Pla de l'Era
>   PR53.   2 Cami dels Poets
>   PR53.   3 Font d'Aixa
>   PR53.   4 Castellet de l'Ocaive

GETTING TO THE WALK:

Take the signposted turning for 'Font d'Aixa' from km5.3 of the CV748 (Lliber to Gato de Gorgos), 3.7km from the junction with the CV745 (Lliber to Benissa). Ignoring all branches, follow the main, intermittently surfaced track toward the mountain, joining the PR at 1.9km. Park at Font d'Aixa (misplaced on the IGN map) at the end of track, 2.4km from the road. The last 100 metres of the track may be muddy, in which case park at the 1.9km point when the track joins the PR.

THE ROUTE:

From the Font d'Aixa reservoir, follow the signposted path up the Barranc de Font d'Aixa, soon crossing the watercourse and climbing onto a terrace. Ignore the signposted path climbing to the left for 'Lliber' and continue along the southern flank of the valley, initially on the level then climbing to a ruin and

A steep climb!

a second waymarked junction (10M). Ignore the main PR climbing to the left and descend past the ruin to recross the watercourse. Continue up the *barranco* on the left bank of the watercourse (our right), passing a second ruin before recrossing the watercourse 100 metres later. Following the waymarks, climb across crumbling terraces (SW), passing directly behind a third ruin (30M). At the end of the next terrace, the way climbs again to cross a small rise before recrossing the watercourse for the last time onto its left bank (35M).

The path now climbs steadily through dense scrub (NW) toward an affluent gully dropping down from the uplands. The route becomes less overgrown as it climbs along the western flank of the gully, then veers round onto the rockier eastern flank and follows a clear way climbing steeply through the rocks for about ten minutes. A longer north-easterly traverse is the harbinger of a gentler climb to the junction with the main ridge path, clearly waymarked and doubling back to the right (1h05).

For the present, bear left and continue in a westerly direction up to a well. Bear left and follow a rough but clearly waymarked route for the final steady southerly climb to the trig-point and ruins of Castell de Aixa (1h20), from where you should have fine views on a clear day. Retrace your steps to the Y-junction at the 1h05 point (1h30) and take the left hand fork along the ridge, which follows a contour on the southern flank of the mountain, passing a dead tree (1h35) before switching to the northern flank below the next small rise.

The path returns to invasive, thorny scrub here, feeding into a slope of abandoned terraces (1h45). After passing a second well, tucked into the bushes on your right, you come to a natural *mirador* below a ruin overlooking the Barranc de Font de l'Aixa (1h50). The path then curves round onto the southern side of the mountain to reach a major crossroads (2h). Carry straight ahead on the narrower path, passing a roofless ruin (2h10) then gradually curving round to the north above a cultivated enclave and a hunting lodge capped with a couple of mini wind turbines, until you come to a clearly waymarked path doubling back to the right (the path carrying straight on leads to the Castellet de l'Ocaive) (2h25).

You're now approaching a major confluence of waymarked paths, so some care is required. Take the path doubling back to the right, crossing a well maintained almond and olive terrace before returning to scrub and descending to a second patch of worked terracing. The path is so badly overgrown here it barely exists at all, but staying behind the clear terrace and pushing your way through the overgrowth, you soon join a broad dirt trail (2h35). Bear right and follow the trail for 25-metres to pass a small ruin. Ignore the red-and-white waymarks up to the right and follow the yellow-and-white waymarks round to the left on a clear path descending (E) to join a concrete track (2h40). Breathe easy as both path-finding problems and prickly scrub are past.

Turn right, then right again 200 metres later, and follow a narrow path descending (W) to a tiny ruin below a stand of mature oak (2h55). The path then crosses a small ridge before descending through an extensive hanger of pine toward a house with an orange roof. The path eventually joins the end of a rough dirt track (3h10) that descends to rejoin the approach track 150 metres from Font d'Aixa.

View towards Montgo

22. Sierra de Segaria

Time:	2h15
Climb:	420 metres
Distance:	4km
Grade:	difficult - this rather depends on how attached to paths you are: if you like a good path, it's difficult; if you're at home hopping about on sharp karstic rock, it's a doddle.
Access:	by car
Short Version:	to the cave

A wild little scramble designed to show you that, no matter how improbable and inaccessible a mountain may appear, there's nearly always something interesting to be found if you look a little closer. Seen from below, the Sierra de Segaria is clearly the preserve of people with a penchant for dangling by the fingertips over sheer drops, with nary a path in sight. Once you get into it, the paths remain negligible, but there are some fine scrambling routes and several cairn-marked ways. Not recommended as a solo excursion. There are too many ankle-turning opportunities on the top to be messing about up here on your own.

ALTERNATIVE ACCESS:

The Monte Pego Urbanizacion is making a fine mess of the mountain's northwestern corner. However, it's tracks and cul-de-sacs do furnish an alternative approach to the ridge.

OTHER WALKS IN THE AREA:

PR58.   6 Tormos Cave Paintings

Anyone who likes this sort of thing will have no difficulty piecing together their own scrambles after a preliminary visit.

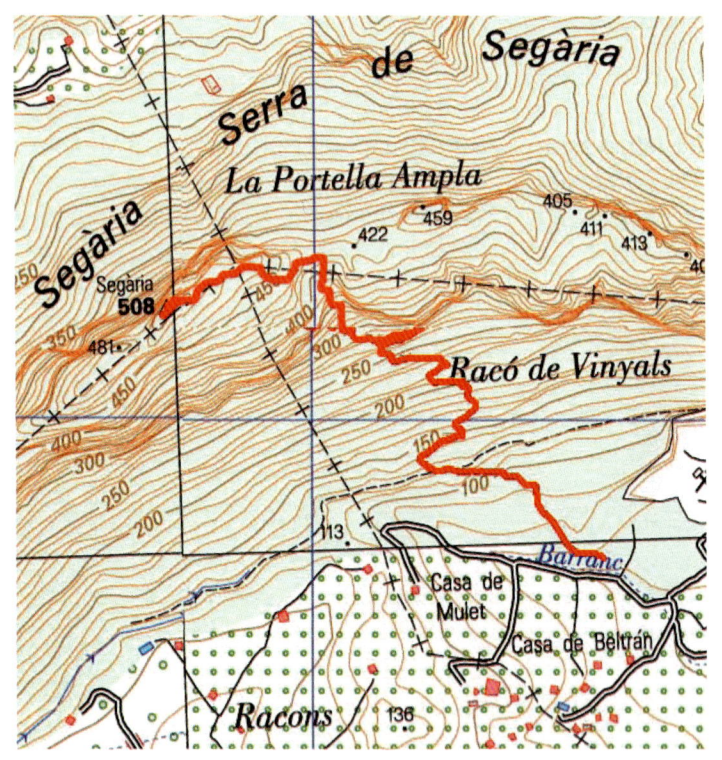

One interesting option might be to contour round the eastern end of the mountain with a view to joining the quarry track back to the starting point. The ridge can also be accessed via the track up to the antennae.

GETTING TO THE WALK:

To reach the start, take the Beniarbeig/Sagra road off the N332 between El Vergel and Ondara. Turn right after 250 metres on an unmarked lane heading toward the sierra and a tall factory chimney. One kilometre after twin tunnels under the motorway, you'll find the car-park for the 'Parc Public Segaria' on your right.

THE ROUTE

From the car-park, take the chained concrete track climbing through the *area recreativa*, at the end of which, very slightly to the left, is a narrow, partially tailored path, the 'Senda Mirador'. The path climbs amid thyme, pine, palmetto, and lentisk to cross a concrete *acequia*, 75 metres after which, we bear right to continue climbing toward the main line of cliffs (10M).

Caves & col seen from near the start

Look up toward the ridge and you will see a whitish band of boulders spilling down below the main col. Slightly to the right, a couple of small caves are tucked into the base of the cliff. There are numerous ways up to cave and col, marked with combinations of cairn and waymarks, and the precise route taken is of little import. All I suggest is that, for a first outing, you stick to one of the marked ascents, make best use of such patches of path as exist, and keep an eye on the objectives of cave and col.

Zigzagging up along the main cairn-marked route, you will eventually find yourself about 100 metres west of the cave, where there's a clear junction of ways (35M). To visit the caves, take the fork climbing to the right and pick your way amid the prickly pear at the base of the cliffs. The caves themselves are little more than shallow indentations in the rock, but are a pleasant little eyrie overlooking the plain to the south (40M).

After a breather, retrace your steps to rejoin the main, waymarked 'path' and follow the white waymarks and cairns (W) into the gully below the col. The waymarked route climbs up the western side of the gully before cutting across onto the right flank for the final climb to the col (70M). From here, the official route heads east onto the Penya Rotja pinnacle.

Alternatively, cross the col to the west and follow a natural, unmarked way winding through the rocks to the first of two small clumps of Holm oak - the only available shade on the ridge. Thereafter, a somewhat precarious progress hopping from one rock to another leads to the trig point (85M). Take care here. There's a very nasty cliff on the northern side of the sierra. Return the same way taking extra care as you descend on the sharp rocks.

Costa Blanca Walks — Sierra de Segaria - 22

The way up seen from the col

Calpe seen from the summit

23. Penyal d'Ifac

Time:	1h50
Climb:	300 metres
Distance:	4km
Grade:	easy, though there's a risk of vertigo and some care is required on the polished rocks
Access:	on foot from Calpe
Stroll:	for a breath of fresh air and a grand sunset view, you could do a lot worse than driving up to the Monte Toix *mirador* behind the Maryvilla *urbanizacíon* to the south of Calpe. Follow the signposts from just south of km166 of the N332. Do drive it, though. The rather hopeful notion expressed by a sign at the bottom intimating this might be considered a PR is risible. Just potter about once you've reached the top.

A classic tourist trail that's such an institution talking it up is like trotting out a cliché, one so superficially redundant it might move your more self-regarding rambler to dismiss the itinerary out of hand. And yet, however commonplace, this rugged headland happily bears endless repetition. It really is an exceptional little lump of rock, clad in lavender, lentisk, buckthorn, scabious, pine, wild olive and several rare endemics, and enjoying unrivalled views of the coast. Moreover, first time visitors may not realize that the rock can actually be climbed. It certainly isn't obvious from a distance and the tunnel that makes it feasible wasn't made until 1918. Until then, the hapless souls sent up to the top to watch for pirates and other nefarious types,

23 - Penyal d'Ifac

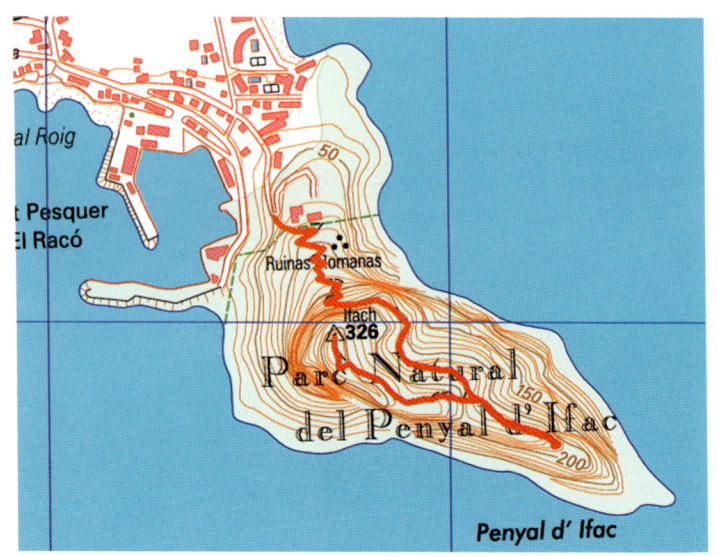

had to make do with ropes. Nowadays the trail is so well worn parts of it are polished to the point of being slippery and there are a couple of vertiginous stretches where moderate care is required. It's not as dramatic as the park authority notices like to pretend, but it's not exactly a flip-flop outing, and sports shoes or walking sandals with a good grip are recommended

GETTING TO THE WALK

I won't insult you by telling you how to get to the walk since the Penyal (AKA Peñón d'Ifach or Penyon d'Ifac) towers over everything else in the vicinity and even the radically near-sighted can't miss the countless signs scattered all over Calpe.

THE ROUTE

From the parking area on the edge of town, stroll up the track past the exhibition centre and the 'Miradores de Levante' turning (5M) to the turnstiles behind the visitor's centre - a counting mechanism, there's nothing to pay. A well-graded climb along a balustraded path leads to the western cliffs of the Penyal and the tunnel (25M).

Beyond the tunnel, another world is disclosed, a realm of seagulls and dizzying drops where anything without wings is at a decided disadvantage. You may wish for wings yourself on the next 75 metres, which are a little vertiginous. Thereafter, ignore the scrambling routes up to the right and stick to the main trodden way as it curves round to an unmarked Y-junction (35M).

Fork left and follow the lower path onto an extraordinary promontory, where you'll find the remains of the old coastguards' hut and fabulous sea views (45M). Retrace your steps back to the main path and follow it inland along the northern flank of the peninsula, passing a second slightly vertiginous stretch (55M), after which a straightforward climb on a clear path leads to the rocks at the foot of the summit (1h01). A narrow dirt path on the left leads to a natural *mirador*, from where a simple clamber across the rocks takes us to the trig-point on the summit (1h05). Return the same way, taking care on the more heavily burnished rocks.

Penyal d'Ifac

View over Calpe

24. Sierra d'Oltà

Time:	2h35
Climb:	400 metres
Distance:	6.7km*
Grade:	easy, though pathfinding can be slightly tricky on the top.
Access:	by car or on foot from Calpe train station
Stroll:	in reverse from the *zona de acampada* to the Ermita and back
Short Version:	the classic circular route continuing on the main track at the 1h10 point or, more interestingly, turning right at the 1h20 point for the 'Ermita Vella'.
Extension:	access from the train station (see 'Getting to the walk' below)

Everyone knows the Penyal d'Ifac, if only from the brochure that beguiled them into booking their holiday, but first time visitors to Calpe may not be familiar with the Sierra d'Oltà, the diminutive table mountain above the rash of *urbanizaciones* behind the town. Seen from below it looks like nothing much at all, but as you approach some interesting crags appear, and once you get into the mountain there are places with superb sea vistas unspoiled by anything that wasn't there a hundred years ago. Above all though, it's an archetype of the sort of landscape to be found throughout the Catalan speaking lands at the end of the Baetic Cordillera, strongly reminiscent of the Balearics and the mountains surrounding Barcelona, a mass of friable marl

---

* My recorded distance differs considerably from the official estimate, which puts a variant of this route that ought to be only marginally longer at nearly 11 kilometres

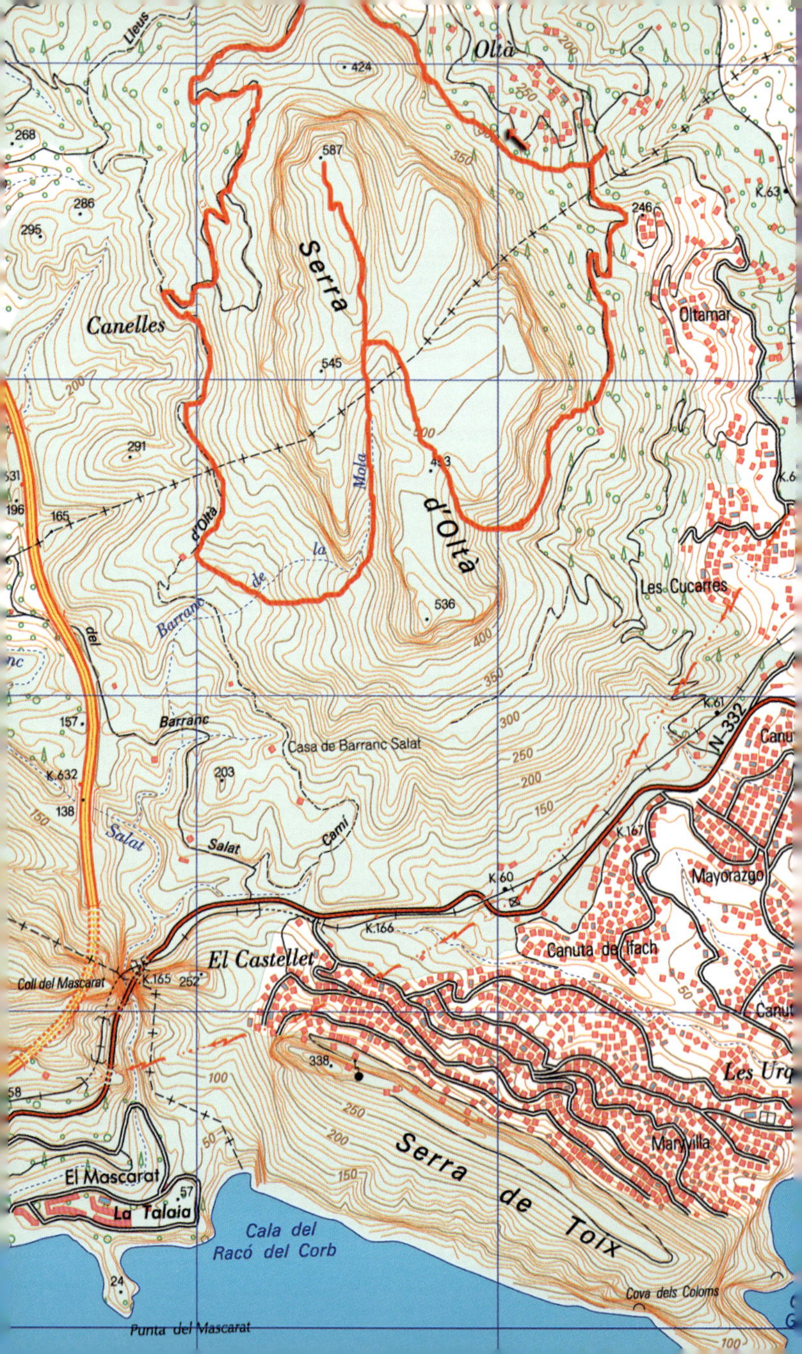
Oltà
Lleus
424
587
268
286
295
Serra
d'Oltà
Canelles
545
246
Oltamar
K.63
291
Mola
433
165
196
d'Oltà
la
de
Barranc
del
536
Les Cucarres
157
Barranc
Casa de Barranc Salat
K.61
N-332
K.632
203
138
Salat
Salat
Camí
K.167
Mayorazgo
K.60
K.166
Canuta de Ifach
El Castellet
Coll del Mascarat
K.165
252
338
Les Urq
Serra de Toix
Maryvilla
El Mascarat
57
La Talaia
Cala del Racó del Corb
24
Cova dels Coloms
Punta del Mascarat

and fractured limestone patched with pine, palmetto, *madroño* (the strawberry tree), cistus, lentisk, thyme, carob, broom, oak scrub and great banks of lavender. Long trousers and walking boots are preferable to shorts and sandals.

ALTERNATIVE ACCESS & OTHER WALKS

Most of the interesting alternatives are touched upon in the course of the present itinerary. Some of these are outlined in a leaflet available from the Tourist information Office, but by no means all. Once you're familiar with the mountain, there are plenty of tiny goat paths, some faintly waymarked, and a few scrambles that merit further exploration.

GETTING TO THE WALK

By car, follow the 'AP7/N332' 'Valencia/Alicante' signs out of Calpe, passing 'Urbanizacion Benicolada'. Drive under the N332 (dir. 'Alicante') and turn left after the 'Centro Comercial' (don't join the main road) for the train station (*Estacion FC* or *FFCC*). Follow the signs for the 'Monte Oltà Zona de Acampada', which is 2.4 kilometres after the railway lines.

On foot, take bus L1 from Calpe to the *Estacion*. Continue on foot along the *zona de acampada* road. Immediately after the railway tracks there are three turnings on the left in quick succession. Ignore these, including the third, which sports a PR sign (our route is more direct), and continue along the road for another 250 metres to the fourth turning, signposted 'Cucarres 2J - 31J'. Follow this road for 200 metres, then turn left after 'Casa Malie' and 'La Torrecilla'. Turn right 25 metres after the end of the tarmac. 150 metres later, ignore a branch doubling back to the left and continue climbing alongside a green fence. Turn sharp right at the next junction to reach the end of the dirt track, after which a waymarked path traverses terraces of pine, joining the track above the *zona de acampada* 550 metres later. This adds an extra 150 metres climbing to the itinerary.

THE ROUTE

From the lower car park take the chained track into the *zona de acampada* and immediately turn left, climbing at each junction to join a track 100 metres later. Bear left and climb to a signposted turning for 'La Canal' (4M). Follow the track to the right until it ends in a turning circle. Continue on the narrow waymarked path (PR plus red dots and blue horseshoes), ignoring a branch descending to the right a few metres later. Turn left when the path joins another dirt track, almost immediately passing a lime kiln, then left again on a narrow path (15M) lined with yellow tipped waypoints.

The path meanders through the pine wood before crossing a rockslide and climbing across crumbling terraces. After passing a cairn-marked branch off to the left (25M), the path broadens to a trail leading to the end of another dirt track at the spot known as 'La Canal', bringing the Sierra de Bernia into view (30M). The blue horseshoe route, which we've been following so far, continues along a terrace on a tiny path that's rapidly disappearing in the undergrowth, while the red route descends to the right 75 metres later. There are other routes to be explored here, including a couple of interesting looking scrambles up to the left, but for simplicity's sake, we follow the track.

Turn left at the T-junction 300 metres later and follow the main track as it curves above the Mascarat Gorge, descending past two branches climbing to the left. Turn left again at the next T-junction (50M) then fork left at two signposted Y-junctions, passing the overgrown pit of an old quarry and the fangs of a ruin - the latter marking the point where another waymarked itinerary joins the main track. 300 metres after the ruin, leave the dirt track and turn left for 'Pou de la Mola / Cim d'Oltà' (1h10).

A waymarked path climbs steadily across patches of erosion, becoming more stable as it reaches stonier ground shortly before another signposted turning at a ruin beside the 'pou' or well (1h20). Turn left into a shallow valley, once cultivated but long since abandoned, then, 150 metres later, fork left again to climb across the terracing into a pine wood on the western flank of the valley - the path on the eastern flank ends in a very obscure but waymarked route leading directly to the *ermita* descent. Above the wood, a narrow path traverses oak scrub to a corral at the head of the valley (1h35), beyond which a clear, signposted path climbs to the cairn on the middle of the three northerly summits (1h45), from where we have fine views of El Montgo, Sierra de Bernia, Sierra Helada, and the Penyal d'Ifac.

Retrace your steps to the corral and turn left to follow a cairn-marked way across the rocky plateau (S) to a signpost indicating 'El Pinet' to the east and (a branch of the path we left after the well) 'La Mola' to the west (2h05). Continue along the cairn marked path to the southeast toward an obvious way off the ridge, soon bringing Calpe, the Penyal, and the Ermita Vella into view. A clear stony path descends increasingly steeply (some care required) to join a dirt track behind the Ermita (2h20). You can either turn right here to rejoin the conventional tour and the short versions or, as mapped, left, passing under the Els Pinets *zona de escalada*. At the end of the track (2h25), a waymarked path snakes its way down to the right to rejoin the main dirt track. If you arrived on foot, a signposted path 50 metres to the right descends back to the train station. If you arrived by car, turn left and follow the track back to the start.

25 - Caves, Capes, Castles and Cliffs   Costa Blanca Walks

The Cap d'Or martello tower

25. Caves, Capes, Castles and Cliffs - four coastal strolls

a. Cova Tallada & Torre de Gerro

Time:	1h15
Climb:	200 metres
Distance:	3.75km
Grade:	medium
Access:	on foot from Denia
Stroll:	to the cave and back

A perfect little walk visiting the Cova Tallada, an abandoned quarry (if only all man-made excavations were so exquisitely fashioned) that's partially underwater when the sea's running high, then looping round Les Planes, the plains below Montgo, to return via a seventeenth century Martello tower, the Torre de Gerro. The official grade for the stroll to the cave is *'dificultad alta'*, which is pushing it a bit, but is presumably pitched at tourists nonchalantly setting off in flip-flops. The actual descent into the cave is a little delicate and should under no circumstances be attempted if a heavy sea's pounding the rocks, but otherwise the walk is easy. That said, flip-flops are not suitable. Sports shoes or proper walking sandals with a good grip are recommended.

ALTERNATIVE ACCESS:

The network of paths and ways on Les Planes can also be accessed from the Carretera del Cap de Sant Antoni (see B)

OTHER WALKS IN THE AREA:

There's a maze of ways and minor paths, mostly unmarked, laid across Les Planes like a web, many of which would make pleasant strolls on a fresh day.

25 - Caves, Capes, Castles and Cliffs   Costa Blanca Walks

GETTING TO THE WALK:

The walk starts at the southern end of Denia in Les Rotes, which is signposted at the start of the CV736 to Xabia. The itinerary begins on a lane climbing to the right a couple of hundred metres short of the end of the road, just past the 'Bar/Restaurante Mena' bus-stop (Line 2). There are two large parking areas at the start of the itinerary. If you're staying in the Los Pinos campsite, which would be a wise move in any case as it's far and away the best campsite on the Costa Blanca, simply stroll along the seafront esplanade until it ends at Platja Arenetes, 150 metres from the start of the walk.

THE ROUTE:

Take the lane signposted 'Torre de Gerro/'Cova Tallada' and climb past the 'San Antonio' flats, quite steeply, until the lane double backs to the right and a signposted track continues south (5M). Follow the signs for 'Cova Tallada', forking left 75 metres later then descending via a short but precipitous staircase onto a narrow corniche path.

The path descends via a second staircase into the Cap de Sant Antoni marine reserve, where it traverses a gently sloping sheet of rock, touchingly but somewhat redundantly decked out with a rope handrail. It then winds along a rough contour above the filigree of volcanic rock embroidering the shoreline before reaching a gully, where a flurry of green arrows indicate the descent to the cave (20M). Conditions permitting, I strongly recommend making the descent. It's an extraordinary spot.

It is possible to continue along the coast to the south, but for the present itinerary, turn right and follow the path climbing along the southern flank of the gully, the Barranco de la Cova Tallada. After a steady climb, an obvious way across the rocks to the left leads to an SL-waymarked (green/white) path along a shallow affluent gully. Fork right at the Y-junction 150 metres later (35M) and follow the red waymarks on a faint way winding through the palmetto scrub, passing a squat white pillar. Turn right at the T-junction 30 metres later (45M) to follow a broad, clear path (NW) lined with lavender and, in early Spring, wild gladioli. The path eventually curls round to Torre de Gerro (1h) and a straightforward descent on the roughly asphalted 'Cami de la Torre' back to the start.

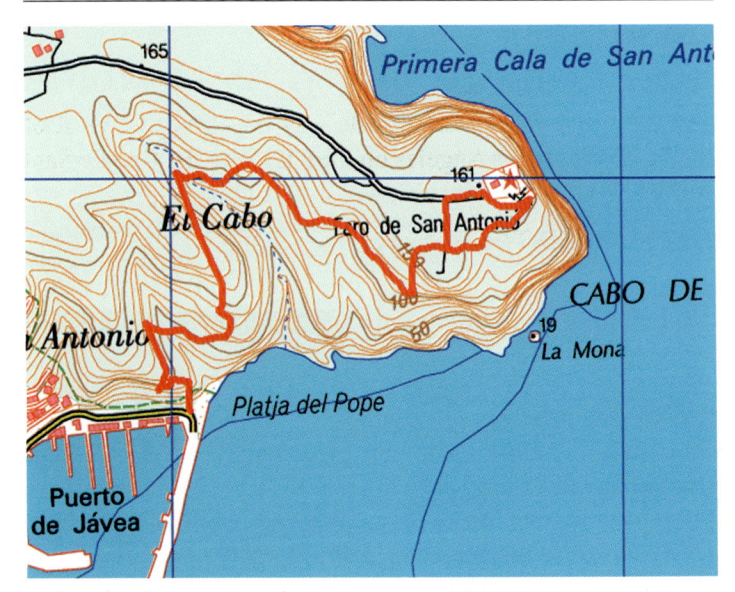

b. Far de Sant Antoni

Time:	1h (rtn.)
Climb:	160 metres
Distance:	3.8km (rtn.)
Grade:	easy
Access:	on foot from Xabia
Stroll:	it doesn't get much strollier than the full itinerary, but if you just want to potter about and enjoy the views, drive to the lighthouse from the CV736.

A fine little outing that, thanks to the folds of the land, instantly eclipses the bustle of Xabia as we climb across peaceful pine clad terraces, following narrow paths hemmed with bushy oak scrub.

OTHER WALKS IN THE AREA:
Ruta des Coves Santes (see text)

SLs are waymarked from a little way East and just West of the Santuario de los Angeles on the Carretera del Cap de Sant Antoni.

GETTING TO THE WALK:

The walk starts at Platja del Tango (AKA Cala del Pope) immediately north of Xabia port, which is signposted throughout the town.

THE ROUTE:

Take the narrow signposted path for 'Ruta Cap de Sant Antoni / Molins de la Plana' climbing behind the Tango Restaurant. Follow the green/white SL waymarks onto a terraced path that winds round the *barranco* behind the *cala* then climbs to a Y-junction overlooking the port. Take the obvious, waymarked fork to the left, following another rough contour round a second *barranco*, passing waymarking plaque No.1 (20M). This is a particularly lovely lost corner and it's hard to believe there are roads less than 500 metres on either side. Just short of the upland, fork right as indicated by a green arrow (30M), passing the signposted start of the 'Ruta des Coves Santes' a couple of hundred metres short of the cliffs (take care) and fabulous sea-vistas below the lighthouse (40M). Return the same way.

c. Castillo de Granadella

Time:	1h10 (rtn.)
Climb:	150 metres
Distance:	2.6km (rtn.)
Grade:	easy-medium
Access:	by car

The approach to this walk is a bit grim as you traverse the sprawl of villas spewed all over Cabo de Nao, but it's worth enduring this dismal spectacle, even for such a short walk, as the Cala de Granadella is idyllic, the castle perfectly situated, and the Restaurante Sur on the seafront serves excellent *tapas*. Top the stroll off with a bathe followed by a bite to eat in the bar and you've got the makings of an ideal half-day out. In spring, look out for poppies, cistus, lavender and gladioli among many other wildflowers beyond my sketchy botanical knowledge. An easy walk, but as ever with these coastal paths, some halfway serious footwear is advisable.

ALTERNATIVE & OTHER WALKS IN THE AREA:

I haven't done any detailed exploration here, but there are a number of interesting looking tracks and trails threading their way into the valley behind the *cala* (now thankfully protected from the cement and scaffolding merchants) and I have been told that it's possible to walk for about an hour along the cliffs from Moraira.

GETTING TO THE WALK:

Follow the signs for 'Granadella' from Xabia along the CV742 and CV7420 then park where the road divides at a no-entry sign 100 metres from the beach.

THE ROUTE

The walk starts on the concrete track climbing to the left of the 'Cami de la Teuleria' and is waymarked with green-and-white SL stripes. Ignore the 'Camino Privado' sign and follow the concrete track as it climbs steeply, passing two branches off to the left. Take the third turning on the left (10M), a gravel track that dwindles to a path 100 metres later as it passes behind a couple of houses. This is where you begin to realize why it was worthwhile dragging yourself past all those ghastly villas, a gorgeous view opening out over the cove and toward the tip of Cabo de Nao as we climb along a balustraded path to a *mirador*. The path then drops precipitously into a gully, after which the balustrades end. It then snakes its way through the scrub before climbing to traverse a narrow band of rock with a rather flimsy rope handrail. Fork right shortly after the narrow band of rock and follow the waymarks and cairns as they indicate a faint route climbing south to cross a small rise before curling down to the modest remains of the castle (35M). Return the same way.

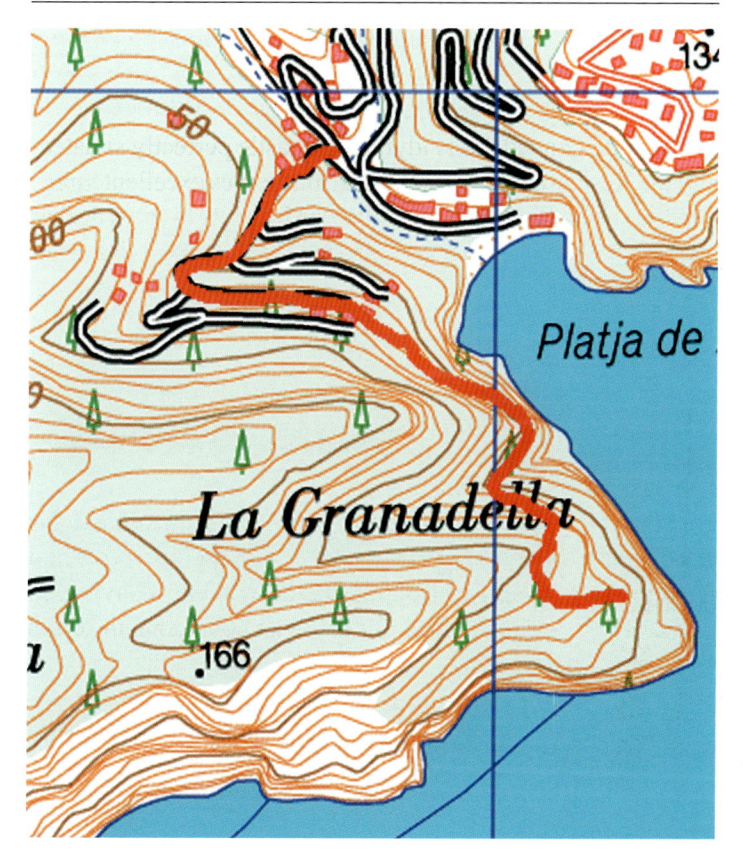

25 - Caves, Capes, Castles and Cliffs Costa Blanca Walks

d. SL51 Torre Vigia de Cap d'Or & Cova de la Cendre

Time:	55M (rtn.)
Climb:	125 or 175 metres *
Distance:	2 or 3km (rtn.) *
Grade:	easy
Access:	by car or on foot from Moraira-Teulada

* Depending on whether you drive up from the beach

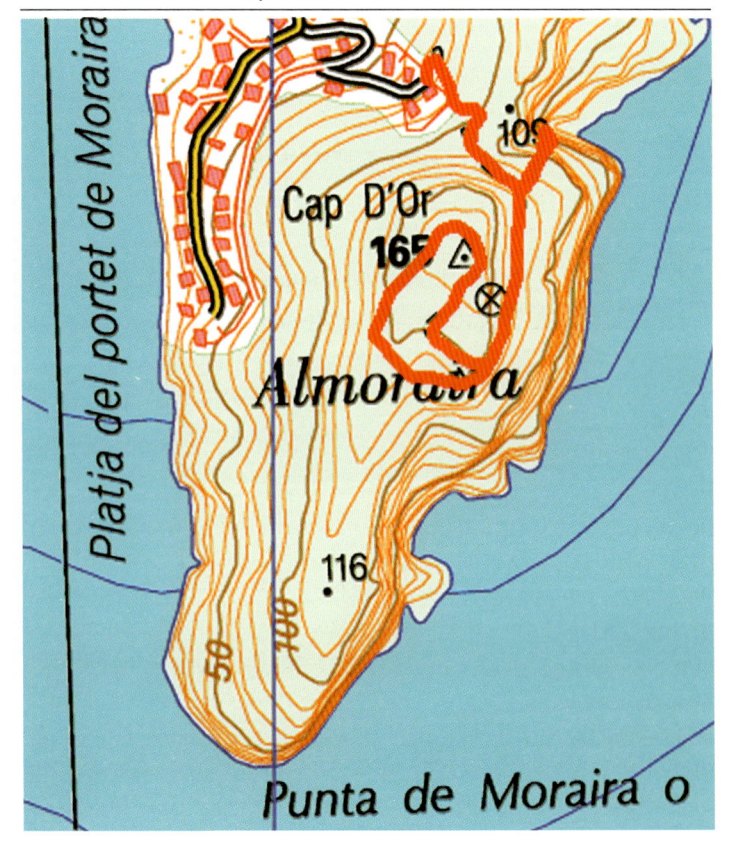

A pleasant stroll of superb views visiting a well-preserved sixteenth century lookout tower on the 'golden cape' of Moraira . The promontory is particularly rich in wildflowers, most memorably mallow, cistus, and wild garlic.

OTHER WALKS IN THE AREA:

SL50 Barranc de la Viuda / Cala Llebeig / Cala Moraig

GETTING TO THE WALK:

From Teulada-Moraira at the northern end of the Moraira bay, follow (on foot or by car) the signs for the *torre* and the green-and-white SL waymarks up to the end of 'Calle Puerto de Alcudia', where the footpath onto Cap d'Or begins.

THE ROUTE:

This stroll couldn't be more straightforward, simply following the clear and clearly waymarked path as it climbs onto the cape, passing three branches off to the left, the third a signposted descent to 'Cova de la Cendra' (10M). We soon arrive on the heights of the cape, where it's worth following the slightly more roundabout clifftop route overlooking Moraira before approaching the *torre (*25M*)*. The cistern passed on the cliff is an *aljub* or moorish style reservoir. Return the same way with the option of descending to Cova de la Cendra, a ten minute diversion that's definitely worth it if you're not of a nervous disposition - there's an awful lot of rock hanging over you!

Ledge path at the start of the descent

26. El Montgo

Time:	4h30
Climb:	650 metres
Distance:	12.75km
Grade:	difficult
Access:	by car or on foot from Denia
Short Versions:	a. Cova de l'Aigua
	b. Cova del Camell via the Cami de la Colonia - also feasible as a cycle ride.

The grand old man of the north, Montgo is a classic example of the sacred limestone mountains strung along the Iberian peninsula's Mediterranean coast, from La Maroma in Andalucia to Sant Llorrenç in Catalunya. The ring of *urbanizaciones* nibbling at its edges suggests the sacrosanct aspect has become a bit frayed with the passage of time, but it remains a magnificent mountain, rising out of the plain in such solitary splendour it's a must-do. There's a slight risk of vertigo, but otherwise the walk is straightforward, only earning it's difficult grade for the rough ground traversed. The terrain is particularly rich in wildflowers, including asphodel, gladioli, flax, lavender and butterfly orchids.

ALTERNATIVE ACCESS:

From the dirt track between kms5&6 of the CV736 between Denia and Xabia, just north of the Xabia firing range (*campo de tir*).

OTHER WALKS IN THE AREA:

See text for the obvious alternatives signposted en route.

Other paths climb to Coll de Pous from the La Pedrera and Jesus Pobre *urbanizaciones*, and to the Cami de la Colonia

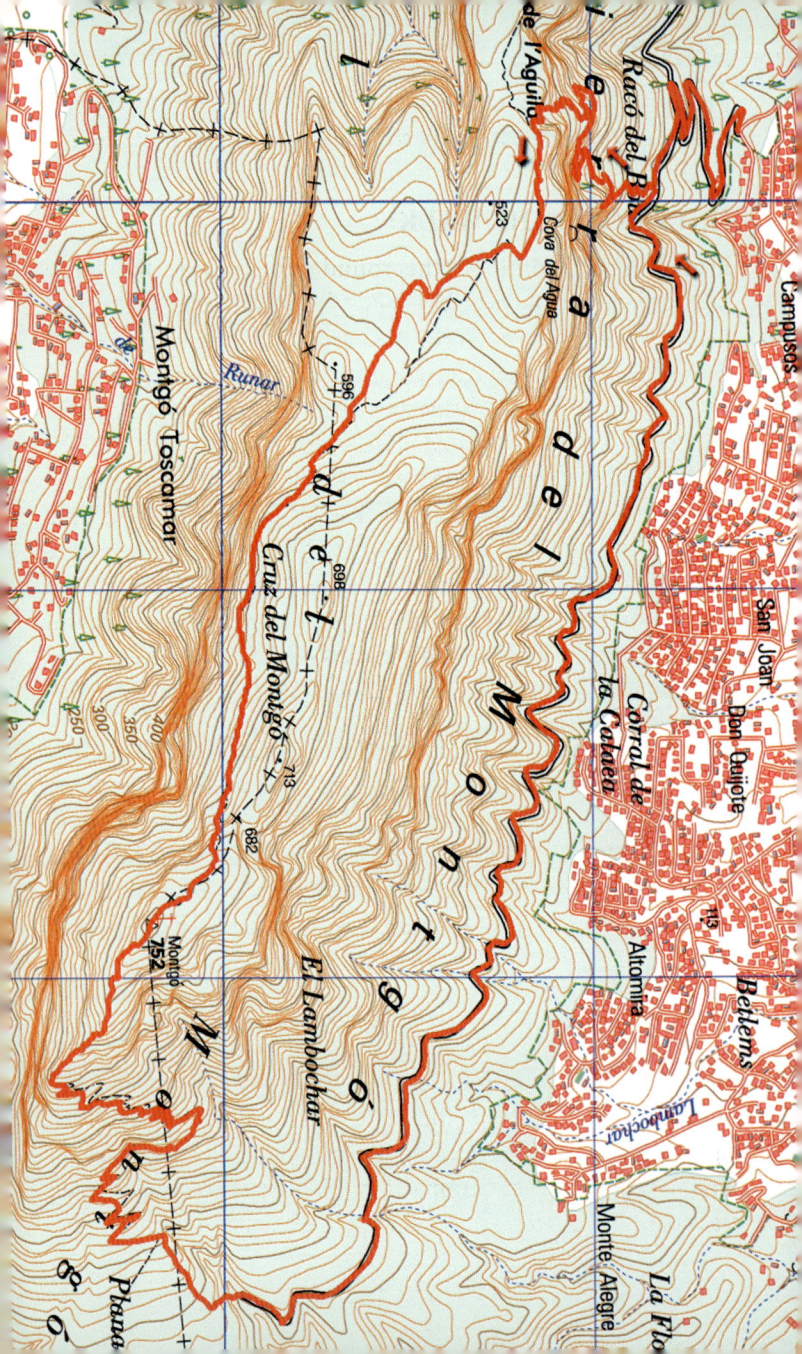

Racó del B...
de l'Aguila
Cova del Agua
523
596
Runar
Montgó Toscamar
698
Cruz del Montgó
250
300
350
713
682
Serra del Montgó
El Lambochar
Montgó 752
Campusos
San Joan
Don Quijote
Corral de la Cercera
113
Altomira
Bellems
Lambochar
Monte Alegre
La Flo
Phan

from the Betlem and Assagador del Pinar *urbanizaciones*. There are numerous strolls to be done from the alternative access point.

GETTING TO THE WALK:

From 'Plaza Jaume I' (the roundabout beside the large 'Mercadona' at the western end of Denia), take 'Avenguda del Montgo' (signposted 'La Pedrera') and bear left after 200 metres on 'Cami Pou del Muntanya' for the 'Parc Natural del Montgo'. Fork left after 1km then right a hundred metres later to pass the recommended parking area at 'Carrer Tantal', continuing on 'Carretera de la Colonia'. The walk starts almost 700 metres after the parking area when Carretera de la Colonia becomes 'Carrer Fenas', at which point a chained off track with a large mapboard, the Cami de la Colonia, climbs to the right. Providing you're not here at the weekend, there should be room to park just beyond the start of the dirt track.

THE ROUTE

Follow the Cami de la Colonia, which is surfaced for the first few metres, as it climbs gently to join the main contour-hugging track on the northern flank of the mountain. The junction is marked with PR152 signposts, indicating 'El Raco del Bou' and the main 'Ruta de la Creuta' off to the right. We eventually join this route, but for a more interesting approach, turn left then fork right 250 metres later for 'Cova de l'Aigua' (15M).

Climbing steadily on a well made path, you'll soon see the *cova* tucked into the foot of the cliffs, betrayed by its balustraded *mirador* and barred gate. At a signposted junction a few hundred metres short of the cave, leave the PR152 and turn right for 'Creuta y Raco del Bou' (25M), following a clear, wayposted path that climbs in easy stages along log-lined traverses. 75-metres after a shallow cave, this route joins the main path from 'Raco del Bou' (40M). Turn left for 'Cim' and climb behind the cave, passing a 10-metre stretch that's slightly vertiginous before zigzagging up to the mountain's obvious 'weak' point, a narrower lip of rock where a natural stony way weaves through the sparse vegetation to a signposted junction with a path from 'Col de Pous' (1h).

Turn left, away from the col, bringing into view the Denia cross (*creu*). Following a clear, unmarked path, head east, initially on the level then climbing onto the back of the mountain (SE) to a solitary pine overlooking a gully - one of three patches of shade encountered on this itinerary and a good spot for a breather. The path continues, rough but clear and marked with the occasional red arrow, curving round the head of the gully before resuming an easterly direction and climbing gently to a col, where views to the south open out.

The gentle climb continues, passing a faint, yellow-waymarked route on the left to the Creu de Denia (1h30). Carry straight on (SE), as indicated by the red waymarks, soon bringing into view the main rise of Montgo. The path is less well made here, but still obvious, the rocks burnished by boots, and red arrows confirm an easterly course after a second faint way descending from the Creu de Denia (1h40). After climbing across sharp karst, you'll reach a clear, stony path and a junction of ways just below the day's second patch of shade, identifiable from afar by another solitary pine (1h55). Bear right here, as indicated by a green waymark, and climb past the pine, 400 metres after which you'll find the Montgo trig-point (2h05). The views from the top are infinitely more breathtaking than the climb.

The descent is via the PR, though it's better waymarked by green-and-white SL stripes and large red dots. It begins beside a tumbledown windbreak 10 metres southeast of the summit, descending a shallow 'stairway' of rock onto a broad ledge path. Slabs of flat limestone and outcrops of sharp karst alternate as we follow a broad spur toward the Far de San Antoni. The walking is rough, but not dangerous and, as long as you follow the waymarks, a relatively straightforward descent leads to a clear, stony path (2h25).

Stick to this path as it traces long traverses down toward the plain between Denia and Xabia, avoiding the shortcuts, which serve no purpose but the promotion of erosion. At the tip of a long, northerly traverse about 500 metres from the end of the CV736 dirt track (clearly visible throughout the descent), PR waymarks indicate a rough way descending to the left (E) (3h) toward the end of the Cami de la Colonia track (also clearly visible throughout the descent). At the second and smaller of two wayposts (3h05), turn left for a slightly skittery descent to the Cova del Camell (the third shady point of the day, accessible via a natural underpass to the left of the path) and the end of the Cami de la Colonia (3h10). All that remains is a delightfully easy stroll along the *cami* back to the starting point.

27 - Penyo Roig from Murla   Costa Blanca Walks

Cavall Verd

27. Penyo Roig from Murla

Time:	3h25 (NB Timings along the ridge are more than unusually subjective given the rough ground and steep climbs)
Climb:	500 metres
Distance:	9km
Grade:	very difficult
Access:	on foot from Murla
Stroll:	to the Ermita then follow the track down to the Murla-Laguar road back to the village.

This is way off the macho end of the walking scale, far and away the most difficult itinerary in the book, featuring a gruelling climb, a rocky traverse above a 100-metre cliff where a fall would be fatal, and a five-metre drop that is a hands-on climb. A rope and climbing experience are not essential (we did it with neither rope or climbing experience, but with a large dog and a good dash of vertigo) but are desirable. I strongly recommend that anyone without climbing experience take a short rope - and a friend! This is no place to be alone. If you're still reading, I should point out that this is also a walk of fabulous contrasts, covering some really wild terrain then looping back to Murla through lovely countryside on quiet country lanes and old tracks. But I can't emphasize enough, it's only for the experts and only in company.

ALTERNATIVE ACCESS & OTHER WALKS IN THE AREA:

The Sierra del Peñón (better known to walkers as Cavall Verd) is most often visited via the PR181 starting in Vall de Laguar and briefly touched upon in the present itinerary. The sierra

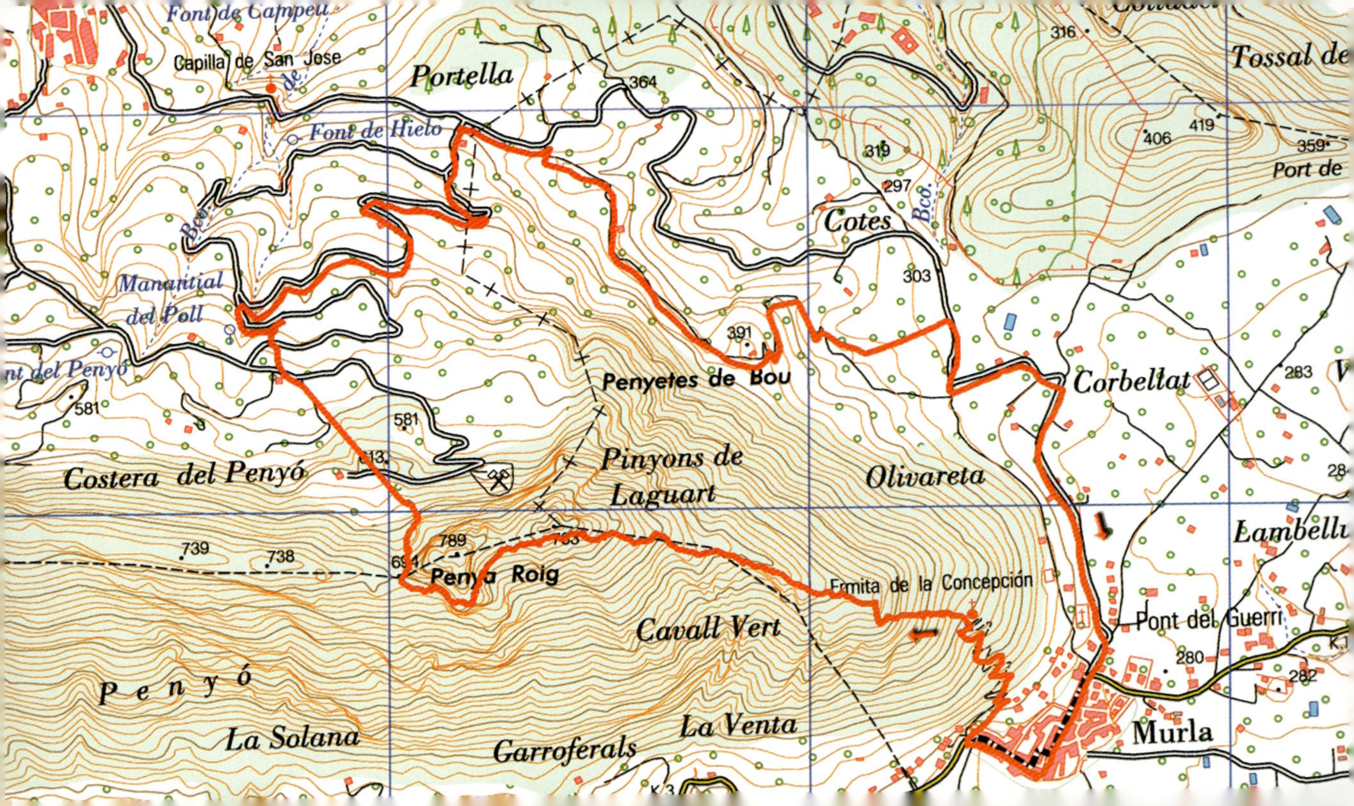

Font de Campell
Capilla de San Jose
Portella
364
316
Tossal de
Font de Hielo
419
406
359
319
297
Port de
Bco.
Cotes
Manantial del Poll
303
391
nt del Penyó
Penyetes de Bou
Corbellat
283
581
581
613
Pinyons de Laguart
Costera del Penyó
Olivareta
Lambellu
789
739
738
Penya Roig
Ermita de la Concepción
Cavall Vert
Pont del Guerri
280
282
Penyó
La Solana
La Venta
Garroferals
Murla

can also be reached via the surfaced track (which partially coincides with the PR) between Benimaurell and the CV720 west of Benigembla.

GETTING TO THE WALK:

The walk starts from the western end of Murla at the end of 'Carrer de la Font' beside the 'Pub Cresol'. The start is indicated by wooden signs for 'Calvario' and 'Ermita de San Sebastian'.

THE ROUTE:

Ignoring a red-and-white GR cross, take the concrete trail climbing to the right and follow the stations of the cross. When the concrete ends, continue on the rough, red-waymarked path on the right, climbing steadily through the pine to the 'Ermita de Sant Sebastia' (15M) (de la Concepcion on the map).

Take the clear path climbing to the left of the *ermita* then turn left 25-metres later to follow a narrow, waymarked trail (red dots) that climbs very steeply across old terrace walls (hands required) up to the cross (35M), where a breather, if not already taken below (this is the toughest start to any walk in the book), will be pretty much obligatory.

Follow the faultline to the north for 50 metres until waymarks indicate a rougher way up to the left along the limestone ridge. The waymarked route follows the ridge to the west and some care is required as you pick your way from rock to rock, taking advantage of the occasional patches of path. The patches of path become more consistent as we skirt the northern flank of the ridge, approaching the first major peak, which is distinguished by a striking outcrop of rock on its right hand side that resembles a rearing sea monster. After crossing a shallow col, a steady to steep climb along the spine of the ridge, mainly but not exclusively on trodden ways, leads to the surprisingly complex folds of the first summit, from the second rise of which we have fine views along the Cavall Verd ridge (1h20).

From this perspective, the main summit is manifestly impassable. It isn't quite, but it's a near thing. Descend to the next col where a large red arrow indicates a faint way round to the left, descending briefly before climbing onto the southern flank of the summit to a junction of waymarked routes (1h40). The main route to the right is strictly for the peak-baggers. Continue along the flank of the mountain, descending on rough bare rock, following the red waymarks toward the third col, taking immense care as you pass above the cliffs that lie ten metres to your left (a fall would be fatal). 100 metres later (it feels like a thousand), the waymarks lead you to the five metre drop, where there's a climber's ring set in the rock for a rope. A large rucksack is a liability at this point, a dog is definitely beyond the pale, and if you suffer from vertigo (as I do), you shouldn't even be here!

Once you've negotiated this obstacle (three shallow ledges make it feasible without a rope) (1h55), breathe a sigh of relief, as what remains gets progressively easier. A rough but not manifestly dangerous way winds through the scrub and rocks down to the main col, where we join the PR (2h). Descend to the right on a blessedly good path to the end of a dirt track. Follow the PR, which leaves the track at the first bend 50 metres later, and descend through a wooded area to join a roughly asphalted lane (the continuation of the track below the col) alongside a small fenced house, the 'Caseta de Adolfo' (2h20). Take the path in front of the *caseta* and continue along the PR as it cuts two long bends from the lane, recrossing the lane after 75-metres and joining it once again 75-metres after

Above the dangerous drop

that. Turn left and follow the lane down past a spring to a Y-junction beside a new house with a swimming pool, where the PR forks left (2h30).

Bear right, leaving the PR and staying on the main lane, which we follow for 1.3 kilometres, ignoring all branch tracks (I tried them all and none serve our purposes) until you reach the T-junction with the road between Laguar and Murla (2h45). Turn right then right again 200 metres later on a dirt track waymarked with red dots. Stay on this track as it winds round the mountain, passing an abandoned cabin (3h) before descending to rejoin the Murla road at the 'Casa Azahar' (3h10), 200 metres from the track up to the 'Ermita de Sant Sebastia'. I suspect the last thing you'll want to do at this stage is climb, so stay on the road for the last kilometre back to the village.

28 - PR.158 Sierra del Carrascal de Parcent — Costa Blanca Walks

Parcent

28. PR.158 Sierra del Carrascal de Parcent

Time:	3h50
Climb:	725 metres
Distance:	13.5km (officially 15km)
Grade:	medium
Access:	on foot from Parcent
Stroll:	Font de la Foia - 250 metres from the starting point, turn right on a tarmac lane leading to waymarked path alongside the dry stream at the bottom of Barranc de les Cabres/l'Alberca/Foya (depending on your map - rather a competitive christening market among the cartographers here), then follow the waymarks to the *fuente*.
Short Version:	from Coll de Rates to the summit. Provided the barrier is up, the track from Coll de Rates to the fire-watch hut *can* be driven in a normal car. However, if you met another car coming the other way on what is mostly a very narrow surface, everyone would be in a hell of a mess. If you chance it and come a cropper, don't start waving the book about and blaming me!

A rugged karstic ridge cloaked in desiccated scrub and embroidered with enough goat paths to keep Pan hopping about for days on end, the Sierra del Carrascal de Parcent is not the place to be in really hot weather, but on a fresh winter's day, when the shady side of the crest may well be permanently patched with frost, the PR158 provides a superb outing. The

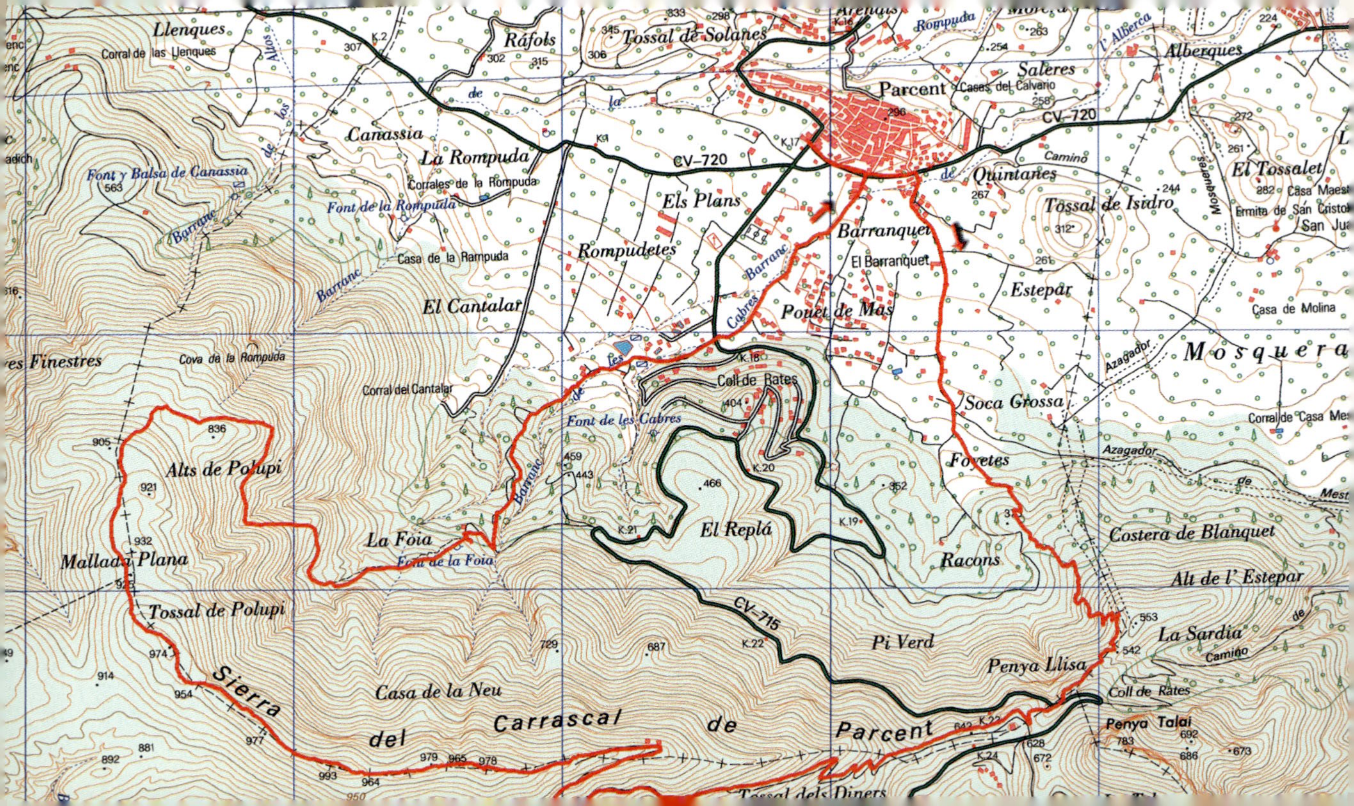

Llenques
Corral de las Llenques
Ráfols
Tossal de Solanes
Parcent
Casas del Calvario
Saleres
Alberques
l' Alberca
Rompuda
Canassia
La Rompuda
Corrales de la Rompuda
Font y Balsa de Canassia
Font de la Rompuda
Casa de la Rampuda
CV–720
Els Plans
Rompudetes
El Cantalar
Quintanes
Tossal de Isidro
El Tossalet
Casa Maest
Ermita de San Cristo
Barranquet
El Barranquet
Estepar
Casa de Molina
Ponet de Mas
Mosquera
Mosqueres
Azagador
Soca Grossa
Corral de Casa Mes
es Finestres
Cova de la Rompuda
Corral del Cantalar
Coll de Rates
Font de les Cabres
Alts de Polupi
La Foia
Font de la Foia
El Replá
Foyetes
Costera de Blanquet
Mallada Plana
Racons
Alt de l' Estepar
Tossal de Polupi
CV–715
Pi Verd
La Sardia
Penya Llisa
Casa de la Neu
Sierra del Carrascal de Parcent
Penya Talai
Tossal dels Diners

mountain itself is not particularly famous, but is surrounded by so many celebrated summits, the views are almost better than from its more eminent neighbours. Waymarks in the valley are not always wholly unambiguous, but when they're really needed on the rough pathless ridge, are precise and unequivocal.

OTHER WALKS

Several short walks and bike rides, some coinciding with other itineraries in the present publication, are outlined in an English language leaflet available from the Vall de Pop Tourist Information Office in Jalon.

GETTING TO THE WALK

For simplicity's sake, we start opposite the chemist on the western periphery of Parcent, at the 'Carrer dels Plans/ Avenguda de Benidorm' bus-stop, near the junction of the CV715 to Callosa (formerly and sometimes still signposted as the C3318) and the CV720 to Castell de Castells. There's plenty of room to park in Carrer dels Plans

THE ROUTE

400 metres along the Alcalali/Xalo road, turn right on a tarmac lane signposted 'PR158 Cumbre Carrascal' (5M). The lane crosses orange groves, becoming a dirt track after 800 metres. 250 metres later, fork left at a signposted junction (again 'Cumbre Carrascal') then immediately right (20M). Fork right at the next junction (25M) and, ignoring a farm track doubling back to the right behind the last of the orange groves, climb ESE on an ancient roughly cobbled mule trail.

Stay on the mule trail as it climbs in easy traverses toward the Alto de Estepar, passing a cairn-marked junction with a path from Xalo before crossing the CV715 at the Mirador de Coll de Rates

(1h05). On the far side of the road, a dirt path climbs for a further 150 metres to the *coll* itself and the 'Berg Café' (1h10).

Turn right and follow the track behind the café as it climbs toward the antennae on the ridge. The track soon runs into concrete, which makes for dull walking, but allows us to dwell on the superb views over the Sierras del Ferrer and Bèrnia, Puig Campana and Monte Ponoig. That said, it's a relief when the tarmac gives way to dirt for the final approach to the antennae, from where the prospect is even superior. Don't stop yet though, as the vista is still better further along, after the track ends in a final spasm of concrete below the fire-watch hut (2h), and the PR continues on a stony path climbing past a trig-point to the first of three small summits (2h05).

Ignore the faint path descending slightly to the left and follow the waymarks along the crest. There are patches of goat path here, but the walking is essentially pathless and, since not all goat paths lead home (at least not to our home), it's vital to ensure you're always walking toward the next waymark, which generally won't be more than 50 metres distant, never more than 100. The way skirts the second summit and climbs almost directly over the third before dipping down to a declivity of rock at the head of a watershed (2h20).

It then traverses the Mallada Plana, a very rough 'pasture' speckled with goat pellets and as many stones as blades of grass, and gradually curves round to the northwest, passing a pile of stones that might once have been a windbreak (2h30). A faint path descends to a Y-junction on a shallow depression, where we fork left (2h35), sticking with the waymarked route as it meanders through the scrub on an increasingly clear dirt path. Fork right at the next Y-junction (2h40), after which the way becomes obscure again, but 100 metres later, a PR-waymarked metal panel on an iron rod marks the start of the main descent to the right (NE).

A clear but rough path cuts through the scrub, bringing Parcent back into view. When this path becomes more obscure at an intersection of goat trails, bear right again (SE), taking care to follow the waymarked route (2h50). The rest of the descent is on a clear but narrow path that curves round to the south to shallow terraces clustered round a watershed (3h), beyond which a sinuous route twists back and forth, crossing a second watershed before joining a dirt track at Font de la Foia (3h10).

Follow the track for 150 metres until it reaches a stretch of concrete, then turn left on a rough trail, actually an abandoned dirt track, descending to the north. The trail dwindles to a path before joining the end of an intermittently surfaced track (3h25). The first house beside this track is home to a large dog that likes people but not other dogs, so if you're walking with a dog, make your presence known to the English owner of the house. Follow the track down to the road (3h35), on the far side of which a track, waymarked at each junction, leads to a path alongside a dry watercourse and a lane back to the start of the walk.

29 - Barrancs de Racons and l'Infern

Barranc de Racons

29. Barrancs de Racons and l'Infern

Time:	2h50
Climb:	400 metres
Distance:	7.5km
Grade:	medium
Access:	on foot from Fleix
Stroll or Short Version:	follow the main walk down to Font Grossa, then turn right after the *lavadero* and descend to the *forat*, the extraordinary hole in the rock through which the PR passes some 700 metres later. Return the same way.

If the full PR147 is La Catedral de Senderismo (The Cathedral of Rambling), then this is the inner sanctum, a variant on the PR that, with the exception of the canyoning route linking this itinerary with Walk 31, provides the most dramatic perspective on these extraordinary gorges.

Unless you have the option of coming as a two car party, almost a third of the itinerary is on tarmac, but it's a small price to pay for the fabulous little path that winds along the flank of the *barrancos*, linking the famous mule trails descending from Fleix and Benimaurell. The PR is popular and can be crowded with large hiking parties at the weekend, so if you can, it's best to visit on a weekday. For obvious reasons, it should not be done after or during heavy rain.

OTHER WALKS IN THE AREA:

PR147 La Catedral de Senderismo (see Walk 31 for additional information)

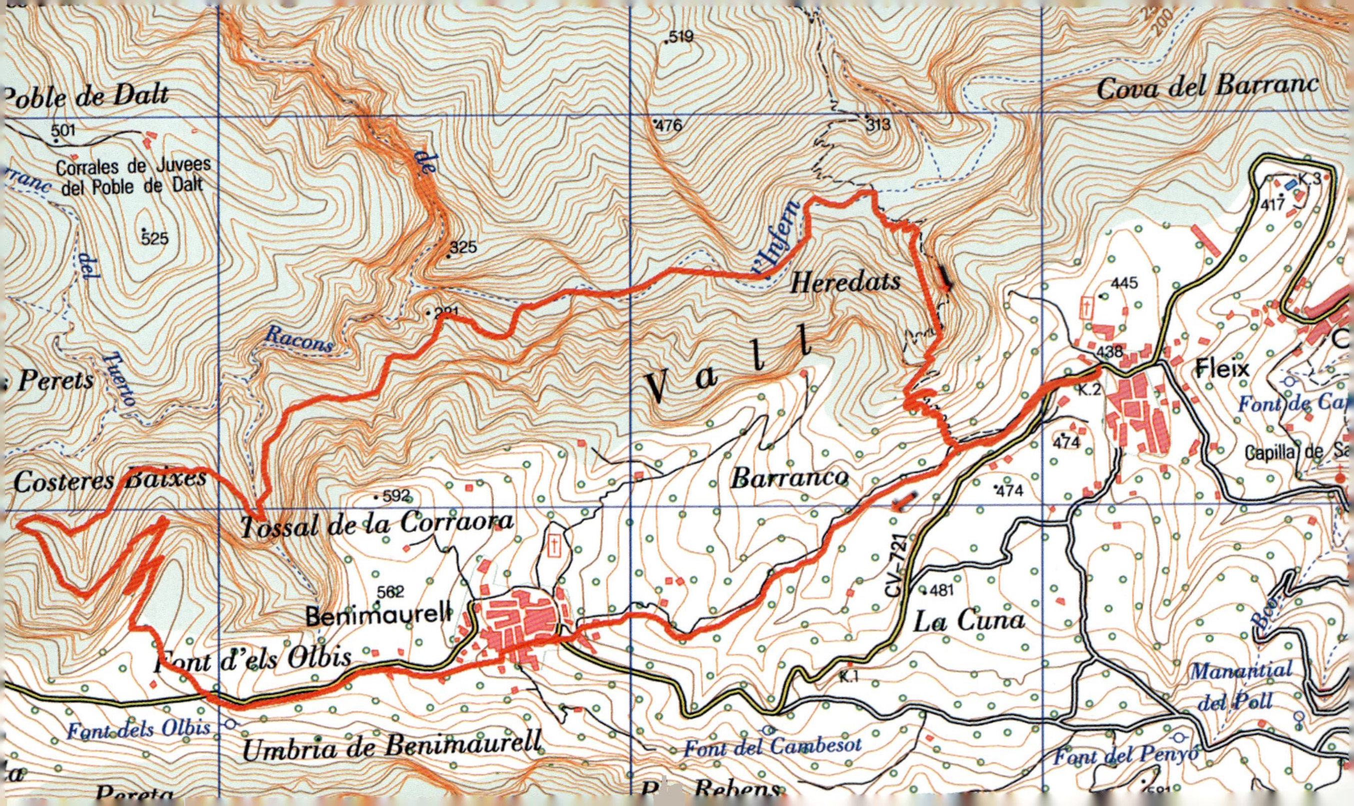
Poble de Dalt
501
Corrales de Juvees
del Poble de Dalt
525
del
Tuerto
Perets
Racons
de
325
281
Costeres Baixes
Tossal de la Corraora
592
562
Benimaurell
Font d'els Olbis
Font dels Olbis
Umbria de Benimaurell
519
476
313
Cova del Barranc
l'Infern
Heredats
Vall
Barranco
CV-721
481
474
474
La Cuna
K.1
K.2
K.3
438
445
417
Fleix
Font de Ca
Capilla de Sa
Manantial
del Poll
Font del Cambesot
Font del Penyo
Rebens
Pereta
200

GETTING TO THE WALK:

The walk starts just short of km6 of the CV721 at the western end of Fleix, where there are mapboards outlining both the PR147 and PR181 Cavall Verd (see Walk 27).

THE ROUTE

Walk up the CV721 and fork right after 100 metres on a minor lane descending to Font Grossa and its *lavadero* (wash-house), 25 metres after which, the short version descends to the right on a narrow, waymarked path. For the full walk, continue along the lane as it descends then climbs steadily to Font de Benimaurell and another *lavadero* (30M). Shortly after the *font*, stairs lead up to the main road which we follow to the right through Benimaurell, continuing on the roughly surfaced lane for 'El Collao'. A steep climb leads past a small *area recreativa*, 100 metres after which the real walking begins on a mule trail branching off to the right, marked with a mapboard and signs for 'Juves de Dalt' and 'Cova Santa' (45M).

The mule trail crosses groves of cherry, almond and olive trees before descending into the Barranc de Racons, from where you can see the continuation of the PR climbing on the far side of the gorge and, off to the right, the way into the Barranc de l'Infern from Juves d'Enmig, used both by the PR and our Walk 31. There's no call to be reading a book here, just enjoy, though spare a thought for people so poor they were compelled to make terraces in such improbable places.

After 1.4km, the mule trail runs alongside an affluent gully (E) before reaching a signposted junction indicating 'Juves de Dalt 25"' on the far side of the gorge (1h10). Leave the PR at this point, forking right to maintain an easterly direction on a narrow, unmarked path climbing slightly before following a contour along a rough terrace, opening up some really grandiose

29 - Barrancs de Racons and l'Infern   Costa Blanca Walks

views along the gorge. The path then descends, quite steeply and on patches of loose stone, to cross a dry watershed below impressive falls, after which it becomes narrower (1h25). After crossing a second dry watershed, we traverse a heavily striated shoulder facing the canyoning route linking this itinerary with Walk 31, at which point the Barranc de Racons becomes the Barranc de l'Infern. Some care is required here as the escarpment on the left as very steep and there's not a lot to stop you fetching up in the bed of the *barranco* if you happened to fall.

Beyond the shoulder, you'll catch sight of Fleix before descending steeply, again on loose stone, into the Barranc de l'Infern. Once in the bed of the *barranco* (1h45), simply follow the cairn-marked paths downstream, crisscrossing the riverbed for about a kilometre until you rejoin the PR147 at the Fleix mule trail, the famous 5000 steps - actually 3800 according to a Spanish source, but I couldn't face counting them myself (2h15).

No prizes for guessing what awaits you now. 1750 steps (the other 2050 ascend the northern wall of the gorge) and a 280-metre climb. In some ways, it would be preferable to do the itinerary in reverse, concluding with a gentle stroll on the road, but preferring to end with a bang rather than a whimper, I opted to describe the walk in this sense. Turn right and follow the trail up toward Fleix into a rockscape so very remarkable it would be an insult to describe it. There's nowhere to go wrong, so simply take your time and take your pleasure, rejoining the outward route at Font Grossa.

5000 steps - maybe?

El Forat

30 - Refugio de la Figuereta   Costa Blanca Walks

Refugio de la Figuereta

30. Refugio de la Figuereta via Travesia el Masset

Time:	2h15
Climb:	275 metres
Distance:	7.6km
Grade:	medium
Access:	on foot from Vall de Ebo

A lovely circuit visiting a lovely refuge and serving as a lovely introduction to a lovely valley. Lovely all round then. 'Nuff said. If you aim to explore further, it's worthwhile spending a little time at the Corral de Saori and Tossals Grau pass 'reading' the landscape to get an idea of other possibilities. The *travesia* is an SL waymarked green/white The rest of the itinerary follows the yellow/white PR58.5.

ALTERNATIVE ACCESS:

PR58 variants 2 & 4 from Pego and Adsubia

OTHER WALKS IN THE AREA:

> PR58. 2 Pego - Refugio de la Figuereta
> PR58. 4 Ebo - Adsubia
> PR43. Les Valls

Another area in which dirt tracks, trails and unmarked paths provide a superb DIY kit. A mapboard at the western end of the village outlines some options, including the attractive Els Tolls stroll.

GETTING TO THE WALK:

The walk starts from the complex of new roads at the eastern end of Vall de Ebo on the track leading to the water treatment plant (*depuradora*), marked with a 20km speed limit sign sporting a PR waymark and wooden boards indicating 'Font del Gili' and 'Barranc de l'Infern'.

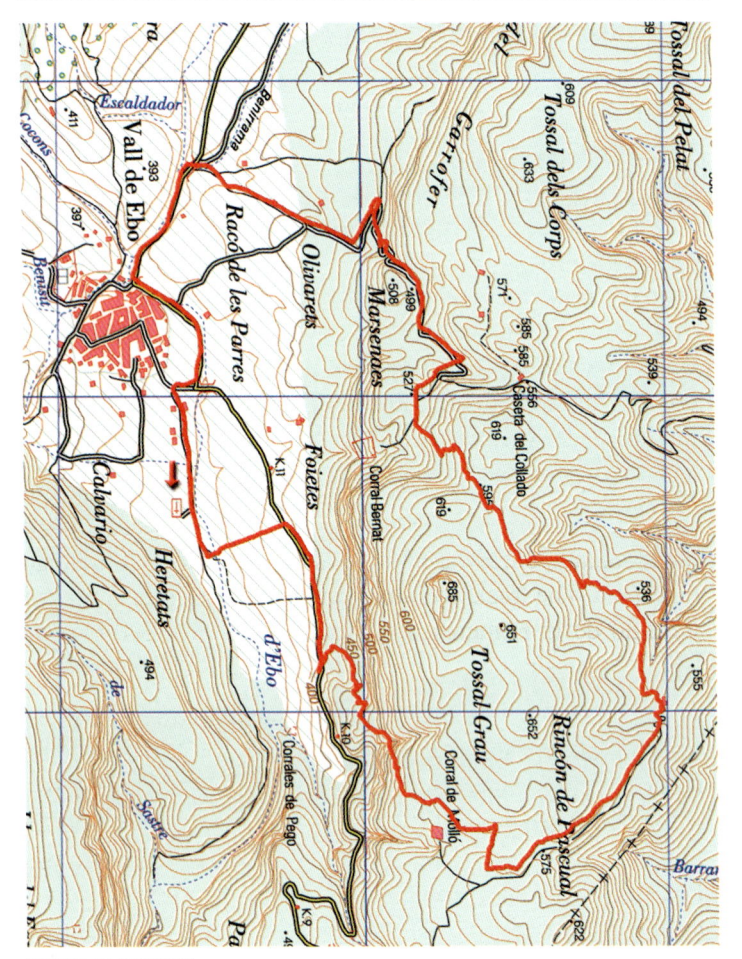

THE ROUTE:

Follow the track toward Font del Gili and, 50 metres after the water treatment plant, turn left on a concrete track signposted *sendero local* 'Travesia El Masset'. Fork left immediately after fording the river to follow a concrete trail, which gives way to a grassy track then a narrow path climbing to the CV712

(AKA the AV431) (15M). Turn right and follow the road for 300 metres until just before the km17 milepost, where a second *sendero local* sign and green/white waymarks indicate a path doubling back to the left (20M).

Shadowing a row of pylons, the path climbs (E) to the overgrown Corral de Saori (30M), beyond which is the *raison d'être* of this SL, a spectacular mule trail zigzagging up through the rocks to a ruined cabin on a rough plateau (45M). 100 metres after the ruin, the Avenc Estret, a 140-metre deep sinkhole, lies just to the left of the path. Turn right here, crossing a shallow terrace, then follow the obvious path as it climbs briefly to rejoin the PR on a dirt track (50M).

Turn left and, ignoring a branch on the left 100 metres later, follow the main track as it curves round the northern side of the mountain, enjoying fine views over Vall de Gallinera and out to sea. The track eventually ends at the idyllic, unmanned Refugio de la Figuereta (www.lafiguereta.org. Tel. 686 090 511 between 9pm & 10pm) (1h05).

To return to Ebo, take the PR-waymarked path descending into the valley south of the refuge. The path follows a contour along the southern flank of the valley then climbs steadily to a junction with an alternative branch of the SL (1h25). Ignore this path and continue on the PR, which soon crosses a pass below Tossal Grau, from where a splendid panorama opens out over Vall de Ebo. After briefly following a contour to the west, the path zigzags down to a rough dirt track heading northwest, away from the village, to join a tarmac lane (1h40). The Castillo de Gallinera/Pla de Misera branches of the PR lie to the right. For the present itinerary, turn left and follow the lane till it rejoins the CV712 at km15, 350 metres from the village of Vall de Ebo.

Font del Reinos

31. Barranc de l'Infern

Time:	4h
Climb:	300 metres
Distance:	14km
Grade:	difficult
Access:	on foot from Vall de Ebo
Stroll:	stay on the track after Font del Gili until it ends in the riverbed. Return the same way.

One of the wildest walks in the book and one of the finest, this itinerary explores the walkable bit of the famous Barranco de l'Infern between the Valls de Ebo and Laguar. Though there's a long stretch (nearly 3km) on a partially asphalted road, this is very much wild walking and not advisable as a first outing or on a hot day. The outward leg follows the PR43 which is rough, narrow, overgrown and, for large rather vital stretches, blessed with waymarking that is at best ancient and inadequate. As a result, I'm afraid a certain amount of time consulting the book is inevitable. By contrast, the return route via the *barranco* couldn't be simpler to describe, since there's nowhere else to go, but it does involve a fair bit of arduous scrambling over huge, water polished boulders. If that doesn't deter you, I can guarantee this will be one of the most memorable walks you do on the Costa Blanca. Long trousers are recommended due to thorny scrub. Not to be done in hot weather, nor during or after heavy rain.

ALTERNATIVE ACCESS:

PR58.6 from Tormos

OTHER WALKS IN THE AREA:

See walk 30

Marsenaes
Corral Bernat
Pla del Molló
Montnegre
Olivarets
Foietes
Corrales de Pego
Racó de les Parres
Benirrama
d'Ebo
Parancho
Solana de
Pla de la
Corral de la
Vall de Ebo
Escaldador
Heretats
Calvario
Sastre
Corral de la Carrasca
Cocons
Benisit
Lloma del Faret
Pla Roig
Barranc
Aspres del Barranc
Ferragut
Planet de la Corona
Pas de Manzaneda
Barranc de Edre
Morral
Tossal de les Manueles
Escalet
Alt de la Manzaneda
Benisit
Coronas
Reginglons de Femenia
Llomets de las Colmenetas
Juvees del Poble d'Enmig
Tomás
Mallada de les Palmeres

GETTING TO THE WALK:

The walk starts as per Walk 30, on the track leading to the Vall de Ebo water treatment plant.

THE ROUTE

Follow the track past the water treatment plant, forking right at the Y-junction 300 metres later to climb past Font del Gili (AKA 'Xili'). 50 metres after the bend beyond the *font*, bear left on a narrow path with a flimsy PR43 signpost ('Les Valls') (15M).

The path descends almost to the bed of the *barranco* then follows a contour leading to terraced fields below a cabin (25M). Bear left, crossing the watercourse via a slightly obscure way confirmed by an old waymark and a waypost. Continue along the left bank of the *barranco* on a grassy path leading (150 metres later) to a small rise, overlooking the end of the dirt track used for the return. Ignore the superficially clearer animal track climbing to the left and continue along the contour in an easterly direction. The path soon curves into an affluent *barranco*, bringing into view the fabulously isolated ruin of an ancient corral, our next objective.

Continue along the contour, following an infinitely narrow terrace and passing one of the few clear waymarks on this stretch just before you enter a wooded area that obscures the views over the *barranco*. Beyond the woods, the PR43 descends through dense scrub to a grassy terrace below the ruined corral (40M). Ignore the clearer traces that climb up the affluent toward the CV712 and fork right, immediately dipping into the watercourse to join a narrow path climbing to the ruin.

Behind the corral the main climb begins, again on a narrow overgrown path, but now with occasional waymarks and little risk of straying off trail. The path weaves up a spur between two watersheds then snakes its way up to a terrace of almond trees below a small house (1h). It continues climbing beyond the terrace, passing immediately to the left of the house (protected by two very large, very loud and very well fenced-in dogs). Follow the dirt track up from the house to the gated but unfenced junction with the Carretera de Barranc de l'Infern (1h10).

Turn right and follow the *carretera* for a little under three kilometres, passing the junction with the PR58 to Tormos after 350 metres. The *'carretera'* is actually an intermittently asphalted track (roughly half the section we walk is surfaced) with five stretches of asphalt. 100 metres into the fifth stretch, at 'Juviles d'Enmig', we join the PR147 and turn right on a dirt track signposted 'Font del Reinos/Barranc de l'Infern' (1h50).

Descend toward the first of the Juviles d'Enmig houses and turn left immediately before it on a broad waymarked trail curving round a lovely almond terrace carpeted with daisies. The trail soon winds into a dramatic descent, passing spectacular overhanging cliffs before zigzagging down to a small spring, the Font del Reinos (2h10), and eventually dropping into the bed of the *barranco* (2h20).

200 metres to the left are the spectacular narrows that make this such a popular *barranco* with canyoning enthusiasts. Ropes and a modicum of experience are required for the full descent, but it is worth making the detour (not counted in subsequent timings) if only for the photo opportunity!

Otherwise, turn right and head up the *barranco*, staying in the watercourse and leaving the PR147, which almost immediately climbs to the left. There's no path here and, to begin with, no clear indication that this is a very sensible thing to do, but you'll soon see small red dots indicating that, sensible or no, it is something others have done before. The gorge narrows dramatically after a breached silt dam (bypassed to the right) and we're obliged to clamber over massive boulders, the looming cliffs curving overhead as if striving to close out the light altogether. There are places in this gorge that never see the sun and, if you happen to be walking in the midday heat, this is the best spot for a break, providing you don't find it all too intimidating. The red dots are more frequent at this stage and are worth looking out for (especially if you're walking with a dog) as they do indicate the path of least resistance through the chaos of rock.

Eventually, we emerge from the main slew of massive rocks (2h50), but there's still plenty of boulder hopping to come as we make our way between banks of oleander and bramble backed by scrub and some still daunting if not quite so menacing cliffs. Shortly after the dentate crash barriers of the CV712 come into view, a narrow path climbs onto the right bank of the *barranco* (our left). Rough by normal standards, this path is as smooth as a politician's lie compared to the preceding antics. After another brief spell in the bed of the watercourse, a second path, this time within sight of the ruined corral, climbs onto the right bank. This deposits us once again in the riverbed for a final stretch on broad sheets of rock before joining the end of the dirt track (3h25) which leads back to the Font del Gili and Vall de Ebo.

Castillo de Gallinera

32. Two small walks, two large valleys: Gallinera & Alcalá

a. Castillo de Gallinera

Time:	1-2h depending on what option you choose
Climb:	350 metres
Distance:	7km
Grade:	easy
Access:	by car or on foot from Adsubia
Short version:	to the castle

A short stroll taking in part of the PR58.4, this linear itinerary is a pleasant introduction to the cherry and almond capital of the Costa Blanca, the Vall de Gallinera. The conventional itinerary takes in the Pla de Misera before descending back to Adsubia, a very logical loop when seen on the map, but very illogical when endured underfoot, as it includes vastly too much time on tarmac. The ascent of the Pla de Misera is, however, a very spectacular drive: from the central square in Adsubia, take Carrer Font down to the *rambla* then follow the concrete and asphalt lane on the far side of the river as it snakes its way onto the plateau.

OTHER WALKS IN THE AREA:

PR58. 1 Caminando por las montañas (Pego)
PR58. 2 Pego - Refugio la Figuereta
PR58. 3 Pego - Castillo de Ambra
PR167 Vall de Gallinera (Beniali)

GETTING TO THE WALK:

From the western end of Adsubia's 'Carrer Principal', take the PR-waymarked lane climbing to the left of the cross and cluster of mail boxes. Follow the PR waymarks along the

32 - Gallinera & Alcalá — Costa Blanca Walks

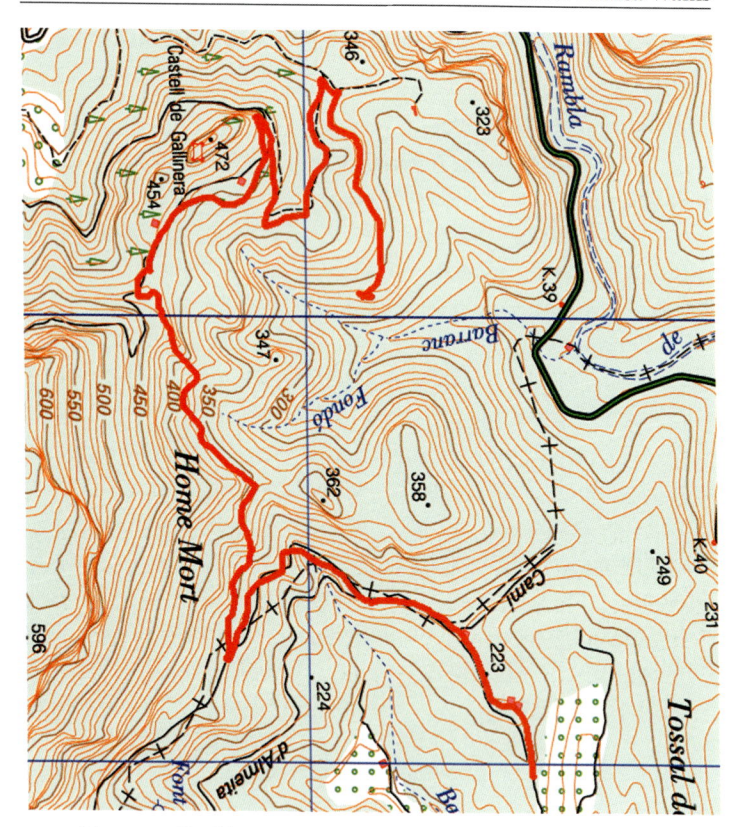

roughly metalled lane and park at the reservoir 1.3 kilometres from the village.

THE ROUTE

From the reservoir, continue on foot up the lane, which becomes a stony track 300 metres later as it passes 'Villa Pilita'. Fork right at the Y-junction 300 metres after that (10M) and continue along the main track as it crosses Barranco de Michel, on the far side of which a much narrower track doubles back to the right below a ruined cabin. Turn sharp right here and, ignoring a branch on the left 50 metres later, follow the track till it ends at the last house in the valley, the somewhat grandiloquently named 'Castell' (20M).

The PR continues on a narrow path, climbing steadily across tiny abandoned terraces to a col at the head of the *barranco*, from where we can see the castle (25M). The path then winds along the hillside, climbing intermittently across fire-scorched terraces to a signposted junction with a rough dirt track (35M). Leave the waymarked route here (the PR turns left for 'Xilibre/ Refugio Figuereta'), and bear right toward the castle, which can be reached by a rough path forking off to the left.

If you want to extend this basic stroll, continue along the track as it curves round a *cortijo* below the castle, bringing into view the westerly reaches of the Gallinera valley. Double back to the right at the first junction (45M) and descend to a small ruin (previously seen from the track below the castle). The track dwindles to a trail descending across partially maintained terracing toward a byre with a corrugated roof. Turn right at the T-junction below an ancient abandoned caravan then right again 50 metres later (55M) onto a narrow track curving round a terrace. The track traverses scrubland before descending onto abandoned terraces overlooking a gully, a pleasantly isolated spot for a picnic if required (1h).

The track becomes overgrown here, but it is *possible* to descend, off-path, into the gully then scramble up its eastern flank to well-maintained olive terraces, beyond which a track leads back to the Villa Pilita. Unhappily, this can't be recommended as it involves very rough walking pushing through so much scorched retama you end up looking like a cross between a coal miner and a muddy Dalmatian. I therefore recommend returning the same way.

b. Penya Foradada

Time: 1h30
Climb: 175 metres
Distance: 5.5km
Grade: easy
Access: on foot from Vall de Alcalá

Vall de Alcalá was one of the great redoubts resisting the subjugation of Moorish Spain and it still has a slightly other worldly feel to it, as if it doesn't quite subscribe to the Johnny-come-lately customs prevailing elsewhere on the Costa Blanca. Even the weather's different, March 2006 seeing such a heavy snowfall all the awnings in the local campsite collapsed under the weight! In this itinerary, we visit the valley's most celebrated monument, the natural stone arch that lends its name to the Sierra Foradada.

ALTERNATIVE ACCESS:

Via the PR43 from Benitaya

OTHER WALKS IN THE AREA:

PR43 Les Valls

The dirt tracks around the village of Alcalà de la Jovada provide the basis for countless winter strolls.

GETTING TO THE WALK:

The walk starts 50 metres to the east of the village limits of Alcalà de la Jovada, shortly before km6 of the CV712.

THE ROUTE

Take the unmarked lane descending toward the water-treatment plant, passing the ruined Moorish hamlet of Adzuvieta, and turn right 50 metres later on a rough track marked with a green arrow. Fork left at the clear Y-junction after 200 metres (10M) and follow a narrower trail, soon passing an ancient PR waymark.

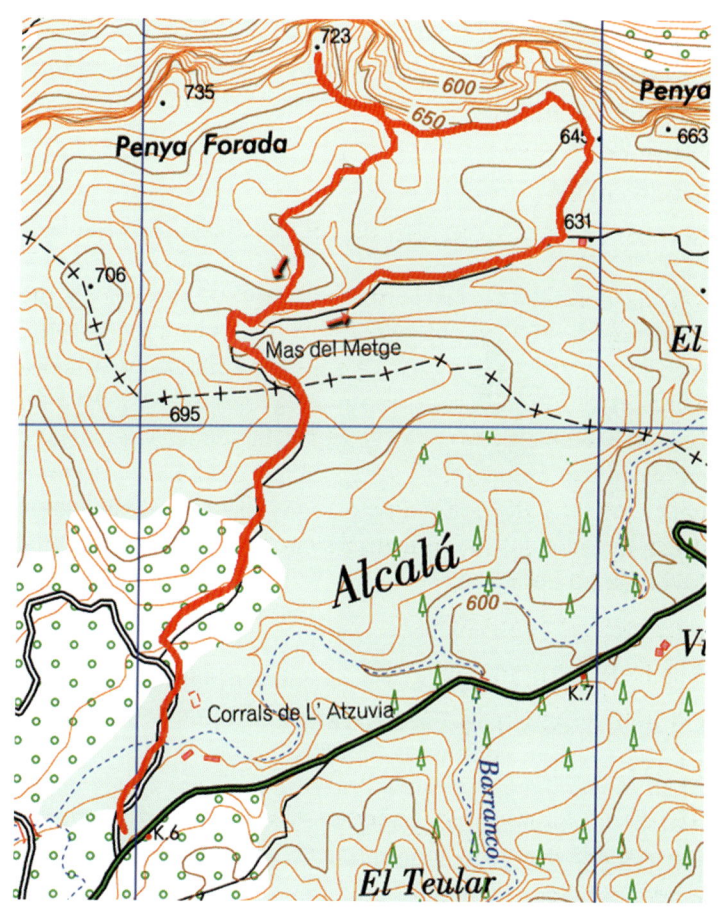

Continue on this trail as it climbs gently amid ragged pine and bushy Holm oak, crossing a small rise before descending into the head of a shallow valley. Stay on the main track as it passes between a ruin and a deep well, ignoring a clear branch climbing to the left 75 metres later (20M). The track follows a contour along the flank of the deepening valley before reaching a junction just short of a restored cabin, from where the *foradada* is visible up to your left (30M).

A Flanagan & Allen moment?

Turn left here then immediately fork right on a narrow path traversing a terrace, on the far side of which a clear way climbs across scrub onto the ridge overlooking Vall de Gallinera, just west of a semi-troglodytic lookout point. Turn left, as indicated by a PR waymark, and follow the PR along the ridge for a little over 100 metres. When the main cobbled mule trail descends into the valley, leave the PR, forking left on a broad red-waymarked trail continuing along the ridge. After passing a small ruin and dipping down briefly, a short but steady climb leads to the *foradada* arch itself (50M). If you're feeling foolish, there's a popular photo opportunity for those imprudent enough to scramble onto the top of the arch.

The return loop is clearly visible from the top. Starting on the nearside of the dip between the *foradada* and the ruin, take the rough trail descending into the small basin to the south. Ignore the broader traces that climb onto two long strip fields leading back to the 30M point, opting instead for a narrower trail curving round the basin to rejoin the outward route at the junction after the well (1h05).

Vall de Gallinera

The Safor track & Benicadell

33. Raco del Duc

Time:	5h30
Climb:	500 metres
Distance:	24km
Grade:	medium
Access:	by car
Stroll or Short Version:	stay on the railway line as far as inclination and fascination dictate.

Threading its way along a spectacular gorge, the Raco del Duc is an abandoned railway line linking the industrial hinterland of Alcoi and the port of Grau de Gandia.

Though not strictly speaking a 'Costa Blanca' walk (it begins in Valencia province), a large part of the itinerary is in Alicante province, and the scenery is far too spectacular to be excluded as a consequence of a purely administrative accident.

Though most of the walk is on drivable dirt tracks and even includes three kilometres on tarmac, the grandeur of the landscape amply compensates for the want of wild walking. We opted for the track traversing the Sierra de Safor (rather than the PR42 path) as it better satisfied the gateway ambitions of the book.

It's an attractive track with fine views, notably of Benicadell, but has recently been widened. Locals assure us there are no plans to asphalt it, but you may care to check with the Gandia Tourist Information Office first, asking if the <u>Sierra de Safor track between the quarry and Orxa</u> is still a dirt track. If it has been asphalted, treat the itinerary as a linear walk along the railway line.

Planícia
Corral del Silvestre
Pla de la Cuta
Pas de la Guarda
Racó de la Tardada
La Guardada
Lloma de les Cartes
Costera del Racó del Duc
Pla de Pere
Corral d'Onofre
Es Albes
L'Arrimall Roig
Salt de la Cavatorta
Racó del Duc
Mas de la Garrofera
Pla de la Cova
Els Cingles
Salt de les Majones
Les Majones
Corral de la Mallada
Pla de les Moles
La Garrofera
Font de la Paguá
Font de la Safor
Corral de la Cova
Font de la Cova
Salt de Surer
Font de la Mata
Coll de l'Ombrieta
Moli de l'Infern
Serpis
Corral de les Mabones
La Solana
Fuenteta de la Serquera
La Cerquera
Penya Roja
Serra de la Safor
Les Parres
Les Mallades
Les Passeres Grans
Corral del Monjo
Corral del Caçador
Corral de les Faseres
Corral de Toni Castellà
La Safor
Riu
Font de Botero
Cova Negra
Racó de la Penya dels Cocons
Casa Martín
Racó del Botero
El Calvari
Mas del Coll del Riu
Font dels Obis
Costera de Galé
Mas de Bassiets
Casa del Fassonar
La Devesa
Font de Bassiets
Lloma de Penya Roja
El Carrascar
La Fonteta
Clot de la Cova
Coveta del Gall
Casa Castellana
Corral de la Sisterna
Racó de Sant
Cova de Gregori
Lloma

The other name of this gorge is Barranc de l'Infern. Take heed! It is not recommended in hot weather. Nor, given that so much of it is drivable, should you do it at the weekend. Ideal on a clear windy winter's day. A torch is advisable for the first tunnel (No.8).

The walk could also be adapted as a bike ride by staying on the tarmac at the start and joining the described itinerary at the 1h20 point.

ALTERNATIVE ACCESS:

From L'Orxa

OTHER WALKS IN THE AREA:

For an alternative stroll, stay on the lane at the start of the walk for another 1.5km until you reach a signposted path climbing on the left to the 'Refuge de Safor'

PR42 Sierra de Safor (see text) - accessible by continuing along the tarmac lane from the start of the walk. The 1h20 point of the present itinerary is reached 3km later. There's room to park at the 1h35 point.

The *via verde* can also be followed from Gandia down to the coast, a route detailed in a pamphlet available from Gandia Tourist Information Office.

The area to the west of Orxa is one of the richest walking areas in the province, with countless excursions around Beniarres, Muro de Alcoy, Cocentaina, and Alcoi.

GETTING TO THE WALK:

From the secondary school (*institut secundaria*) at the western end of Villalonga, take the minor road running parallel to the Riu Serpis, signposted 'Reprimala / La Safor / Raco del Duc'. The walk starts at a signposted junction just after the quarry 3.5km from Villalonga.

33 - Raco del Duc

Note: the first four kilometres of the walk until the junction with the PR can be driven; however, the first 1.9kms are narrow and rough, and passing places are limited.

THE ROUTE

From the quarry junction, take the track descending to the right for 'Raco del Duc', forking left after 'Casa Rosa'. The track joins the railway line above two abandoned generating plants and a shrine to the Senén Pla virgin, an image of whom was said to be found floating *upriver* in 1708, *away* from Villalonga as it happens, but a sufficiently impressive feat for her to be adopted as the village's patron saint (15M).

Turn left into the first tunnel (No.8 as counted from Alcoi), at the far end of which is an idyllic enclave. Tunnel No.7, short and requiring no torch, debouches onto an orange grove (25M). 100 metres after Tunnel No.6, our itinerary joins the PR42 (40M). For shorter walks, continue along the railway line. For the full itinerary, turn left for 'Font de la Mata/Cim de Safor', ignoring the faint path into the bushes and following the PR waymarks directly over the rocks to the south.

After 50 metres, a clear, but narrow path runs along the edge of a rough terrace before climbing steadily through invasive oak scrub. There are several obscure stretches clarified by cairns guiding us to a watershed (50M), shortly after which a signpost indicates the 'Barranc de la Parra salt' - the dry waterfall off to the right (55M). Directly behind the falls is the Font de Serquera *área recreativa* and an alternative route up to the 1h55 point. For the main walk, stay on the PR, bearing left to continue climbing steadily (E), recrossing the watershed and passing a large cairn before a clear path across an olive grove leads to a partially metalled track (1h05) (accessible by car if you continue along the lane after the quarry).

Follow this track as it climbs past houses and cabins to a signposted turning doubling back to the right (1h20). Turn right for 'La Safor' and follow the roughly metalled lane as it climbs to 'Casa Tarsan', behind which we turn right on a dirt track, signposted 'Cim de la Safor' (1h25). This is the track we follow all the way to Orxa, so the following is purely for the purposes of pacing progress and identifying alternative walks:

- The track passes a mapboard and signposted path where the PR42 climbs on the left to the summit, snowpit, and *'finestra'* or window in the rock (1h35).

- After dipping down to cross the head of Barranco de la Parra, the track passes a signposted turning descending to the right for 'Font de Serquera' (1h55).

- The track then levels out amid plantations of pine and almond before being rejoined by the PR42 at a signposted junction with a track on the left to 'Font dels Olbits' (2h05).

Shortly after passing a second turning on the left, this time for 'Font de Bassiets' (2h15), the track becomes a tarmac lane. Follow this lane (not too bad if it's not too hot) as it descends through the barren lands behind Orxa. After two kilometres, the PR descends directly into Orxa, but since our itinerary continues along the road to the northwest, it's easier to stay on the lane for the remaining 700 metres until it runs into the *rambla* below the village (2h55).

Turn right and follow the CV701 for another 700 metres until it crosses the Riu Serpis. Immediately after the bridge over the river, turn right on a narrow waymarked track (3h05), passing to the right of the abandoned paper mill and ruined castle, Castillo de Perputxent. The track meanders amid mostly vacant *huertas* before joining the old railway line (3h15). Turn right and put the book away, as our itinerary now simply follows the railway back to the start. For the purposes of pacing progress:

- 250 metres after the first house on the left and just before the first main stand of pine, a narrow path doubles back on the right to Fuente Botero (3h30).

- Tunnel No.4 (3h40).

- Pass two rough branches climbing to the left (3h50).

- Fork right at a major Y-junction (4h10), staying on the waymarked route as it descends to a bridge below the main Fabrica de Luz, briefly abandoning the railway line which is cut by a collapsed bridge.

- Tunnel No.5 (4h25).

- Rejoin the outward route (4h35).

The main gorge